MW01294044

TREMENDOUS

TREMENDOUS

The Life of a
Comedy Savage

JOEY "COCO" DIAZ

with Erica Florentine

BenBella

BenBella Books, Inc.
Dallas, TX

This book is based on the notes and recollections of Joey Diaz. Some names and personal details have been changed or omitted to protect the privacy of individuals. In passages containing dialogue, quotation marks are used when the author was reasonably sure that the speaker's words were close to verbatim and/or that the intended meaning of the speaker was accurately reflected.

Tremendous copyright © 2023 by Joey Diaz

BenBella Books, Inc.
10440 N. Central Expressway
Suite 800
Dallas, TX 75231
benbellabooks.com
Send feedback to feedback@benbellabooks.com

BenBella is a federally registered trademark.

Printed in the United States of America
10 9 8 7 6 5 4 3

Library of Congress Control Number: 2022045486
ISBN 9781637742617 (hardcover)
ISBN 9781637742624 (electronic)

Editing by Rachel Phares
Copyediting by Leah Baxter
Proofreading by Jenny Bridges and Isabelle Rubio
Text design and composition by PerfecType, Nashville, TN
Cover design by Brigid Pearson
Cover photography by Troy Conrad Photography
Printed by Lake Book Manufacturing

Special discounts for bulk sales are available. Please contact bulkorders@benbellabooks.com.

To my mom . . . I did it.

CONTENTS

INTRODUCTION

I grew up seeing firsthand what it meant to hustle. My mom never skipped a fucking beat. I tried to take a leaf out of her book, and I'll be real with you, my life became a shitshow for a while when my warped motivation for hustling led me down some dark paths. (Like, once on a coke bender, I got so paranoid I called the cops on myself . . . *multiple times*. Oh, and I've also kidnapped a guy. But we'll get to all that later.) I didn't intend to fail on my mom's wishes for me—to be a decent American man—or to fail on my hopes for myself, but along the way I did. I failed miserably.

When I eventually found my stride with comedy, things started to take a turn for the better. My past failures became less important—less defining of my character—and connecting with my audience was all that really mattered. I'd been doing stand-up for years before I figured out the special sauce. One day I woke up and it just *clicked*. I started telling stories about the crazy shit I'd done in my life, not knowing how it would land. I was shocked (and grateful) to find there were people out there who liked hearing them. I grew a fanbase that quickly felt more like family to me than anything else. I was their Uncle Joey.

If you've listened to my podcast or seen or heard me anywhere else, you know my life stories aren't always pretty, but that was my point in writing this book. I want to tell you as much as I can: the bad mixed in with the good and the funny, with some names and minor details changed to protect people's privacy. For anyone who might be going through some shit right now, my hope is that when you're done reading this, you'll know for sure that you can get past it. You can find happiness and success in your life, trust me. I was lower than low. In fact, I was barely a functioning human at certain points, addicted to crime and cocaine, but I came out the other side.

Don't get me wrong, this book isn't a sob story. Parts are sad, yeah, but you need to hear that to understand me as a whole. We all have our crosses to bear, and some stories from the early parts of my life are mine.

As I'm writing this introduction, I'm in my home in New Jersey. My beautiful wife, Terrie, is here too, and she's hanging out with our daughter Mercy, who I love more than anything. Later we'll all have dinner together as a family. Then, I'll smoke some dope and make some notes for tomorrow's *Uncle Joey's Joint* podcast. I'm living a dream—*the* dream I always wanted to live.

My Uncle Lazaro has told me a lot about my father, who died when I was a little kid. Uncle Lazaro said my dad and I were similar in lots of ways. We looked similar and had the same mannerisms, but mostly, we were born to hustle. It seems I had two parents with that mentality. Sometimes I reflect on how I got to where I am now. And it's really that *hustle* but with the right motivation. What you'll notice is that once I found my motivation for changing my life—comedy—I just kept showing up. Day after day. Night after night. I showed the fuck up, I practiced my skill, and I stayed focused, even when other parts of my life were shaky. The hustle nearly killed me in the early parts of my life, but the hustle also saved me in the end.

My advice to you is to do the same. Just keep showing up. Just keep hustling, and doing it with the right intentions. Go ahead and take a leaf out of *my* book (besides the hard drugs and robberies, let's say), and make shit happen!

And for anyone who isn't going through tough times and picked up this book to have a little fun, let's fucking do it. I got a lot of fun shit to tell you.

In fact, sitting down to write this book, I realized there's so much to say—so much I want to share with you guys—that I could write twenty books based on my life experiences alone. *It has been a hell of a ride*.

Enjoy, cocksuckers.

Childhood

Want to See a Dead Body?

n the winter of 1984, I was waking up most mornings in a rusty rocket ship in North Bergen, New Jersey.

I was twenty-one years old, an orphan, and homeless. The rocket ship was a piece of playground equipment in the park I used to go to as a kid, and since the top was mostly covered, it gave me at least some kind of shelter during the freezing cold nights. I'd climb up to its second floor—my penthouse—and squeeze my adult-sized body in there, no blanket or anything, just my winter coat and whatever other clothes I had on my back. I had nothing to my name and nowhere to go. I'd exhausted all my options. For the last couple of years, I'd been causing problems and burning bridges one by one with the people closest to me. Drugs, robberies, guns being pulled . . . you name it. No one wanted me to stay with them, and I couldn't blame them.

I wasn't a bad guy at all. I'd just become a junkie and couldn't break out of the cycle. Those mornings waking up inside the rocket ship, I'd replay how I'd let it get that far. How did I end up here? I guessed it was a combination of circumstance and upbringing. Don't get me wrong about my upbringing—I had a devoted mother. I'd just been exposed to a lot of shit kids should probably never see.

My mom, Denora Valdez—who went by the alias Sophia Cecillio— immigrated to New York City from Cuba with me when I was three years old. My dad, Manolo, had just died from accidently snorting heroin, and we couldn't get my sister out of Cuba with us, so it was just me and my mom.

My mom had a bar in Union City, New Jersey, called El Reloj, which means "the clock" in Spanish. Union City was the second-biggest Cuban community in the United States after Miami, so we fit in nicely there. That was good, since we spent most of our time at her bar when I was really young, even though we lived in New York City. At the same time, my mom was also running numbers—a type of gambling that was illegal at the time—out of a dry-cleaning business in the Bronx. This woman would do anything to make a buck, especially when it came to gambling. She was an absolute degenerate gambler. And one badass motherfucker.

My mom was about five-foot-two with black hair regularly pulled up into one of those beehive hairdos. She was one of those hard-ass Cuban women you hear about but have probably never witnessed in action. She took shit from no one . . . and I mean *no one*. The reason for the alias was that she'd stabbed someone with a broken bottle back in Cuba and needed a clean name when we moved. The guy she stabbed had raped her sister, and that was exactly the kind of shit my mom was not going to tolerate.

This woman was as tough, if not tougher, than the men around her. She always had their full respect, too. When she walked into the room, she was not only their equal in terms of money, she was equally as street-smart—if not more. She was not scared of anything.

My mother didn't believe in day care, so when we first moved to the United States, she brought me to the bar with her every day and then back again at night. Every day started the same. She'd have a couple of drinks at home, and then we'd head to the bar to get it ready for its 11 AM opening. Once we got there, my mom would mark a quarter with red lipstick—I don't remember exactly why—and play Tony Bennett's "I Wanna Be Around" on the jukebox. Then, she'd put out a drink and a smoke in honor of my dad in front of the big portrait of him she'd hung on the wall. Every day, like clockwork.

The inside of the barroom always smelt the same—a mix of cigarettes and booze—and it was always dark in there. The bar itself was black and made of wood. It was long, like thirty-five feet, with a TV at the end that only played sports, and the seats were covered in velour. My mom had a pinball machine in there, and a shuffleboard table, and there was a pool table in the far back of the place. She also had one of those old pay phone booths—one that you could go into and close the door behind you to make a call.

One of my jobs at the bar was to work the audience once they got there. I was like a dancing monkey putting on a constant show. When I wasn't jiggling my ass, I was greeting the customers—mostly a mix of Cuban regulars—one by one, chatting with them about their day. Since I knew most of them, and their spouses too, I was able to bring in a few bills whenever I'd see one of the married guys hitting on women who were *not* their wife. I'd go over and start busting their balls until they'd slip me three dollars to go the fuck away. The next time it happened, I'd up the stakes and ask for five dollars. Eventually, I'd make up to twenty dollars a pop just to mind my business, and if they didn't pay, I'd kick them in the shins. If cops ever came by and saw a kid dicking around in the bar, they didn't say shit about it. That's probably because *they* had a deal with my mom that benefitted both sides.

In between working as the in-house entertainer, I got a chance to take a nap on the cot my mom set up for me in the back room. But soon I'd be back at it. I was initially a nervous kid struggling to learn English, but I gained my confidence quickly at the bar. I had my other little jobs to do for her there, too. As a toddler, you'd find me restocking the shelves in the back, mopping the floors, or cleaning the bathroom. I remember being only a few years old and sticking my hand in the box in the women's bathroom and pulling out some bloody period stuff, not knowing what it was. The bathroom part of the job was horrible, but I was already making some money, so it was all good with me.

The real eye-opening stuff came when we took our midday breaks from the bar and headed to Zoraida's. Zoraida was my mom's best friend and a huge drug dealer in Harlem. The two of them knew each other from Cuba and got really close when my mom and dad rescued Zoraida from an abusive husband out in Chicago. My mom and Zoraida ultimately showed me the true meaning of friendship, but first they showed me that it was normal to do coke in the middle of the day.

The two of them would rip lines every afternoon during our short stop at Zoraida's. I still don't really know if there was any other purpose of us going there every day other than for the two of them to show each other what clothes they'd recently bought, do their blast of coke, and throw back a drink together.

Once those two were done, my mom and I ran our errands for the bar. We'd make a quick stop at the record store to get some new 45s, and we'd go put in our food orders for the bar's kitchen. For lunch after, we'd grab Chinese food or, if we were feeling fancy, a steak. In the summers, we'd always make time for a Mets game in the afternoons so my mom could place a bet, sit out by right field, and throw chicken wings at Rusty Staub.

Then, we'd go check in on her dry cleaning business, aka numbers running operation. This is where the real gambling went down. She'd place bets on the day's number and check on her staff, and I'd make sure nobody went thirsty by bringing out cold beers from the back fridge or the local bodega. Yeah, "bolita," as we called it, was illegal, but who was going to stop my mom—especially when the cops came in to play, too. We'd make time for a quick dinner before heading back to the bar for the night shift. I'd pick right back up where I left off—doing my little jobs and entertaining the evening crowd. It was tremendous.

I didn't get a rest from performing much, since on Tuesdays—my mom's only night off—she always had her ladies over to our apartment on the Upper West Side. They'd play cards, drink, and smoke pot or whatever, and I'd sit there, eyeing up her friends. I love women so much now because I was raised around women. I've always felt comfortable with them.

I'd be exhausted after a while and ready for bed, but the second I'd want to go to sleep they'd start screaming, "You can't go to sleep, Coco! Dance for us!" (My dad called me Coco as a baby because my skin was as white as the inside of a coconut, and the nickname stuck.) And right then and there is when my real show of the week would start. They'd feed me a shot of tequila, put on "L.A. Woman" by The Doors (my mom loved this song), and stand me on the table, where I'd dance around in my tighty-whities, gyrating my hips like Elvis. They'd be clapping and my mom would shout, *"Dale jamón!"* (which means "give 'em ham"). After the fast part at the end, I'd literally pass out, and Mom would carry me to bed. When I woke up in the morning, they'd all still be awake playing cards and drinking. They never wanted the party to end.

For me, the partying had to stop at some point. I was forced to quit drinking with them around the age of four after I hit the bottle too hard one night. I'd noticed my mom would take a shot of wine every night before she went to sleep. She told me it was good for her digestion. It was that Italian wine she'd always have, the one with the fat, rustic looking bottle. It looked cool, so I had to try it. One night when she fell asleep, I drank a whole fucking bottle. When she woke up and couldn't find me anywhere in the house, she called the cops. Everyone was frantic until they found me in a closet covered in puke.

Don't get me wrong, my mom wasn't the only one involved in making my early childhood less than normal. She eventually came to the conclusion that I needed a male influence. She figured maybe my godfather, Gaby, would be the perfect companion for me.

Gaby was a solid motherfucking dude. He was also a good-looking dude, like a Spanish Dick Van Dyke. Same haircut and sideburns and everything. Gaby and my dad had been close back in the day, so hanging out with him was really like hanging out with another father figure. It was great because Gaby was always happy, chill, and giggling from constantly smoking skinny joints. He was excellent to be around. Gaby started spending time with me every Saturday, and we'd go see Disney movies like *The Love Bug*. But he got sick of that kids' stuff real quick.

One day he pulled me aside.

"Listen kid, I can't do this anymore," he said. "What do you say we go to see one of my movies?"

I agreed, and off we went to the James Bond movie, *On Her Majesty's Secret Service*. I'd never seen a movie like that. I mean, I was only a few years old. I fucking loved it.

"And if you don't tell your mom, we'll keep going to see these movies," Gaby said afterward.

So that's just what we did. Every time we'd go out, it would be one rated-R movie after the next. I was learning so much. After we saw *Dirty Harry*, Gaby brought me to a nearby restaurant to get a steak and a potato and asked what I thought of the movie.

"It was really good," I told him, shoveling a forkful of beef in my mouth. "The guns were crazy."

"Oh yeah?" he said. "Here, put your hand out under the table."

Before I realized what was happening, Gaby put a gun in my hand. There I was, barely old enough to use a steak knife, and I was holding a gun for the first time.

"Same gun as in the movie," he said.

A Smith & Wesson .44 Magnum. The huge gun dwarfed my small hand.

"What do you think?" Gaby wanted to know.

And, of course, I fucking loved that, too.

———

When it came time to start school, I was fucking terrified. Fitting in as a Cuban kid wasn't easy. My mom raised me to be independent, and yeah, I'd seen some shit, but being up against the American kids was something I didn't think I was ready for yet.

For the first day of school, my mom got me a Beatles lunchbox to help me fit in.

"Whatever happens, don't let anyone take your lunchbox, Jose Antonio," she said, holding it up for me to see.

At first, I had no issue here. It was a pretty cool lunchbox. Then she started to fill it up. Before I knew it, she filled it with a whole Cuban meal: a steak, rice and beans, a thermos of milk, a hand towel, and to top it off . . . jewelry beads and a statue of a saint.

How the fuck was I going to fit in like this?

"I don't want to take this to school," I yelled. "I want to be an American. Americans eat hot dogs!"

I was convinced back then that the more hot dogs I ate, the more American I'd become. My mom couldn't care less what I had to say about it, though. I was going to school with that thing. So there I went, off to make my first impression, lugging an eighteen-pound lunchbox.

When it was time for lunch, I wasn't ready to risk the embarrassment. I grabbed the lunchbox and bolted out of the school to toss it in the lake at Central Park. On my way to dump it, I saw what I'd been dreaming of . . . a Sabrett hot dog cart. I scarfed down three hot dogs in a row. I felt myself becoming more American with every bite.

As I was about to toss the lunchbox into the water, these three little dirty fucks came up to me ready for a fight. They must have been ten or twelve years old—at least a few years older than me.

"What's in the lunchbox, cocksucker?" one of them asked.

I stared back at all three of them knowing damn well it would be easy to hand it over and not start any shit. But that wasn't our Cuban way, you know what I'm saying? I kept hearing my mom's voice: "Don't let anyone take your lunchbox." Now, I was determined to keep this lunchbox, come hell or high water. I refused to hand it over.

"None of your fucking business," I told them.

They jumped me, and before I knew it, they popped open the lunchbox and spilled everything out onto the ground. One of them got ahold of the thermos and cracked me in the head with it. It all happened too fast. Blood was pouring down my face, but I still had the lunchbox in my hand and managed to get away.

In that moment, when I heard the glass of the thermos break against my head, something in me changed. Yeah, I'd always had that Cuban rage deep inside of me, it was in my genes. But now I was dead set on never getting my ass kicked again. These motherfuckers fueled the fire for me to get tough, like real street tough. I'd seen Bruce Lee in the movies and, damn, did that immigrant give us all hope. If Bruce Lee could come in, a fish out of water, and kick everyone's asses, I could too.

I got my mom to let me take karate lessons so I could learn to really defend myself, too. To further help the cause, I started spending a ton of time away from our apartment down on 88th Street, where all of the well-off pussy kids lived, and started roughing it up further uptown on 148th.

One Hundred Forty-Eighth Street in New York City is where Beva, my Santeria godmother, lived. When people hear "Santeria," they tend to think of voodoo and witchcraft, but it's really not about that at all, especially for Cubans. It's deeply engrained in our culture and actually heavily woven into Catholicism. In Cuba, 70 percent of the people are Catholic, and 100 percent practice Santeria. Santeria is all about energies. A lot of times when a child is troubled in any way, Cubans will get that child involved in Santeria to help balance out their energy.

As a kid, I was a sickly little fuck. Nosebleeds all the time, sleep-walking, asthma, constantly in and out of the hospital—the whole nine. On top of that, I hadn't been dealing with my dad's death well at all. After he died, I couldn't understand that he could be there one minute and gone the next. Every time someone walked through the door, I'd look to see if it was him. Between constantly being sick and being haunted by my father's death, people suggested that my mom bring me to a Santeria doctor to see if something spiritual could help me.

Beva was a beautiful Afro-Cuban woman, and she took on the role of figuring me out. She taught me the old-school version of Santeria, which was specifically focused on health. It wasn't until later, when Santeria started being heavily practiced by Cuban cocaine dealers, that it began "getting dirty" in some sense. As a teenager, I'd come to see that *dirty* side of Santeria when it was practiced in our house by a criminal named

Tati, but I'll get to that story. For now, when I was just a kid, Santeria was pure gold, and hanging at Beva's to get trained in its practices was great for my health.

Meanwhile, the company I was keeping up there on 148th Street was great for my toughness. The first day I spent at Beva's place, I ran into the group of local kids that hung out around her block.

"Hey, you want to hang out with us?" one of them asked me.

"Yeah," I said, excited to make new friends. "What are you guys doing? Stickball or something?"

"Nah," they said. "Want to see a dead body?"

The crew took me down to the area between Riverside Drive and the Henry Hudson Parkway, a seedy spot up there at the time. As promised, right there in plain sight, with the Hudson River flowing in the background, was a dead man's body. The guy had been shot and now his fat, swollen body was just lying there, covered in bruises. I'm not sure how long he'd been dead, but you could smell him from twenty feet away. The cops hadn't done shit about it, either. It took another day or so after I'd seen it for the cops to even find out about the dude's corpse, and only then did they rope off the area to investigate.

I tried to play it cool in front of my new buddies, but inside I was thinking, "What the fuck?" Down where I lived, the craziest thing I'd seen was a parent slapping their kid around (this was the 1960s, mind you). Now I was getting to see what New York City was *really* about.

These kids were fucking savages. They didn't care about anything. In their area of the city, they saw shit like that all the time. I was jealous that they were so rough and tough and secretly wished my mom and I didn't have the money to live where we did so I would be tough like that, too. I wanted to be just like these guys. These were *my kind of people*.

I could tell my balls were getting bigger right away from hanging out with them. They were doing anything to hustle money, and hanging around them was giving me a different edge. Every day, they'd offer to sweep up in front of businesses and take out the garbage for a small fee. If the shop owners refused, garbage would spill out on the walkway, windows would break, accidents would happen. It was already obvious to me that I had to act dirty if I was going to fuck around with these kids, so that's exactly what I did. I started joining in on the hustle.

I was into building model planes around this time, and there was a stationery store near Beva's that sold the models and the glue to put them together. Every time I went there, there was always this guy hanging around outside who would give me thirty cents to buy him a tube of glue. I didn't know why he wanted the glue, but I did it for him, no questions asked.

One day the store owner said to me, "Listen, that guy out there, do not buy glue for him. He's snorting it. We don't sell it to him anymore."

I came to learn this glue dude was a Vietnam vet who'd been injured there and was now on disability. Whenever he got a check, he'd spend the entire thing on glue: ten boxes of glue at a time. He was living with his mother nearby and would throw huge glue parties there. One day I was taking the garbage out at Beva's, and I saw him hanging out by the garbage cans sniffing glue from a paper bag. Best part is, when he saw me, he tried to hide it, but the paper bag was stuck to his hand. From then on, we called him Sticky Charlie.

Seeing glue was a hot commodity for Sticky Charlie, I knew the game I needed to play. I got money from my mom and bought a giant box of glue.

"Hey, turns out glue went up to fifty cents, Charlie," I told him the next time I saw him. "I'm the new glue man in town."

And that was that—extra money in my pocket just like nothin'. Like I said, we hustled. I learned to never miss an opportunity, even at the age of six.

2

The Stepfather

Not long after I met my stepfather, Juan, I watched him shoot a guy in the leg. We hopped in the car afterwards, went down to the Hudson River, and tossed the gun in the water together like a family. We never spoke a word about it after that.

Juan was a no-nonsense guy and a man of a thousand weapons. When it came to guns, he had them hidden everywhere. Not just in our house, but everywhere he went. If he was going to a friend's house and knew he'd be back there in the future, he'd bring a gun and hide it somewhere in their house, just in case he ever needed it.

My mom knew Juan from when they were young, back in Cuba. They grew apart over time, mostly because Juan had got caught running numbers and was locked up in Sing Sing prison just north of the city. With my father gone, my mom started visiting Juan more often, and from time to time, she'd bring me along too. She would pack my pockets full of coke and heroin before passing me over to sit on his lap. I had no idea what they were up to. All I knew was that Juan was a nice dude who sent me drawings of Bugs Bunny in the mail. After Juan got out of jail and did his stint in a halfway house, he came to live with us in our 88th Street apartment. He and my mom eventually got married in 1969, when I was six years old.

Juan was about six-one with salt-and-pepper hair and the ruggedness of Charles Bronson. He was not flashy by any means—he wore the same clothes five days a week—and it was on purpose. The last thing he wanted was people thinking he had money. He was constantly petrified the FBI would track him down for illegal gambling again, and he needed to stay one step ahead of the cops. This is why he was always, and I mean *always*, sober and with his wits about him. Sure, he sold powder in jail to get by, but he would never drink or do drugs. He was ultraconservative.

He'd been married before, and it bothered him that he wasn't able to save that marriage and that he had a daughter he wasn't allowed to see. But it helped him, at least a little, that he was able to start a new life with us and resume the role of husband and dad. It's almost like he got a do-over. Later in my life, I'd be able to relate a lot to what he was going through at that time.

Juan came into the picture at the perfect time in my life. I'd had Gaby around as a male influence, but I was still spending a lot of time with the ladies. My mom was still worried that I'd grow up to be soft, despite all our efforts. Plus, with no grown man of the house, it felt good to welcome Juan in. Not that my mom needed any protecting, but having him around upped the ante. If no one fucked with my mom before, sure as shit no one was fucking with my mom with Juan there. Juan did not play around. If he wanted to hurt you, you were next to dead.

Once, when I was off from school for the summer just a few months after my mom married Juan, she and I headed to a Mets game. Anytime we got in a cab to go to a game, we needed to take the route *she* wanted to go—and she'd let the driver know from the second we got in the cab that she wasn't fucking around; follow her directions. It was important to her that we be there for the entire game, including batting practice. Being late wasn't an option.

On this day, this particular cabdriver decided to ignore her and take a "better route."

What a stupid motherfucker.

He ended up hitting traffic, and my mother went nuts. The two of them yelled at each other before she finally made him pull over and told him she wanted her money back. When he said no (another big fucking mistake), she got me out of the cab. For whatever reason he went to get out too, and my mom shoved him back inside and grabbed the keys right out of the ignition. In the process, she cut her hand.

My mom knew just how to work this angle. She told the cabdriver that she was calling the cops, walked over to a nearby pay phone and—while she was actually calling Juan—she started wiping the blood from her hand onto her face. By the time she turned back around to the cabbie, she looked like fucking Carrie.

See, this was a badass bitch. This lady knew there was a payday coming.

"The fucking cops are coming," she screamed at him. "Stay where you are, asshole."

This schmuck actually believed her and decided to just sit there and wait. And again, *what a fucking mistake*.

Ten minutes later I saw exactly what I'd expected to see . . . a Mustang pulled up, and out popped Juan from the passenger seat. When he saw my mom's face covered in blood, he turned white as a ghost.

Juan didn't speak great English, so he took me with him up to the cabdriver to translate. I went back and forth with them trying to explain the story, and I could tell Juan was not having it. He let go of my hand, nudged me back a little, and just started whaling on this guy like I'd never seen. Juan's hands never stopped moving and I stood there with my jaw on the ground, watching the show.

Fuck Bruce Lee. This wasn't some fake movie shit. This was real life, motherfucker. It was beautiful.

"My stepdad *runs* this city," I remember thinking.

Puerto Rican Nelson, one of my mom's business partners, had shown up with Juan, too. He got out of the Mustang and stood by my mom and me, watching it all go down. Weirdly enough, the cops actually did come a few minutes later. There I was thinking, "Juan is fucked," but this guy was a master at what he did.

As the cops started to walk over, Juan slipped his hand to his waist, and I freaked. I thought he had a gun and was going to kill them. But he went into his pocket, cupped his hand, and greeted one of the cops with a smooth handshake. Then he and Puerto Rican Nelson slid in front of the cops, blocking their view of the cabbie, and started a conversation as if nothing was happening.

Suddenly, Juan's English was somehow perfect. They talked for a while about the weather and the Mets, and then one of the cops finally said, "Hey, what's wrong with him?" and pointed to the cabbie rolling around on the ground.

Juan replied, "Oh, I don't know . . . he fell or something."

The cabbie was lying there, whining, beaten to a pulp, and the cops just left him there. That was it. New York City in the 1960s, I'm telling you. It was something different.

———

My stepfather's weapons definitely weren't limited to just guns and his fists. I've never seen someone more powerful with a can of pepper spray.

But his specialty was the straight razor. He was known to slice guys right in the ass.

Juan hated being around drunk people, so when people were acting too drunk, he'd lose it. The night he shot the guy in the leg, we were all at a Santeria party and Juan was just sitting there in the corner, minding his own business, reading a Spanish romance novella. Some drunk guy we knew named Nico—who everyone called Nico Picadillo because he loved eating picadillo, a Cuban chopped meat dish—kept busting Juan's balls. His patience wore thin pretty quick.

"You got a fucking problem?" Juan finally said to this dude.

All it took was Nico to say "yeah" back to him, and it was over. He went and grabbed this house's hidden gun and the two of them took it outside. Juan squared off with the guy right in the middle of the street. Nico raised his fists. Juan shot him in the leg.

So this was my new dad. I liked seeing my mom happy, and since I didn't really remember much of my own dad, this guy was *it* for me. Juan taught me things like how to put VO5 in my hair and grease it back all nice. He was smooth, and he was teaching me how to be smooth, too.

Juan was what they call Abakuá, an ultra-macho faction of Cuban men who never eat pussy and refuse to be in the same room as a gay man. This guy was slick, though, and let me tell you something—he was a hard nut to crack. It's always the dudes with very few words to say, the ones who are just sitting back listening and watching all the time, that have the most power. His sense of humor was minimal, and it could change very quickly. The fact that he was so serious most of the time made him very intimidating to people, and rightfully so.

He had a strong belief system, and part of that meant taking his Cuban heritage very seriously. For example, in Cuba, December 17 is one of the most sacred days because it's San Lazaro's day. San Lazaro is the patron saint of dogs and one of the most important spiritual figures in our culture. For Cubans, this means do not—under any circumstance—fuck with a dog.

I saw Juan defend this belief firsthand. We were driving through the Bronx and saw a guy on the sidewalk hitting a dog. Juan stopped the car and honked the horn, yelling at him, "Don't fuck with that dog."

When the guy responded, "Fuck you, mind your own business," Juan didn't even pull the car over—he just put it in park right in the middle of the street and jumped out. He threw the ultimate beating on this guy. He smashed his face in and kicked him over and over until the guy could barely move.

Then he got back in the car and we drove off like nothing. We never spoke about that one again either.

3

Fighting *Is* the Answer

We ended up moving from New York City to New Jersey after my mom tried to stab my childhood bully's dad.

Yeah, despite my growing toughness, I had a bully. His name was Rudy the Haitian and his main move was screaming, "Immigrant!" at me at every fucking opportunity, and I was tired of hearing it. One day I finally got the nerve to fight back. As the inevitable word crossed his lips, I laid it on him. Motherfucker was done for.

I guess his dad didn't like the beating I gave his son because not long after, he showed up at our apartment building and pinned my arms back while Rudy ripped on me. Then, he brought me inside to my mom, but that poor bastard had no idea about my mom.

Rudy's dad started threatening her that the next time I tried to fight his son, he'd stab the both of us. Hah! My mom grabbed her biggest kitchen knife and went at him, chasing him around the building. This woman hauled ass in her slippers, screaming in Spanish that she was going to kill him for hurting her son. When the cops got there and confronted her, she denied having a knife at all, and our neighbors backed her up.

The cops let her go, and Rudy and his dad forever knew not to fuck with us again.

Our landlord was mad, though. It was the straw that broke the camel's back after a few months of us causing problems. (Like when I'd start fires so I could try to piss them out, or when my mom brought a live goat up the elevator for a Santeria party, or that one day I was killing time by throwing vinyl records out the window and accidentally hit someone in the head, and they needed to get stitches. We didn't think these things were *too* awful.) After the incident with Rudy's dad, the landlord kicked us out.

We actually weren't very upset to go. My mom was tired of making the commute back and forth to her bar every day; I was tired of asshole kids like Rudy; and Juan—he was fine with us going, too. It was May of 1973 when we packed our stuff and made our way to North Bergen, New Jersey.

We moved into a bi-level house made of all brick on a dead-end road. The house had a bay window in the front that always had the curtains drawn shut for privacy—and another small window off to the side of the front door that my mom used for pouring out hot water on Jehovah's Witnesses. Our house also had a big yard with an above-ground pool, and there were tons of other kids my age that lived on our street—all in all, a dream for me.

What I found out pretty quick in Jersey was violence remained an important part of life, and it continued to be encouraged by parents—not just mine. On our first day living in North Bergen, my mom forced me to go outside and make friends. She dressed me up in my finest suit, all ironed and white from head to toe with freshly shined shoes, a hat, and a gold chain. I looked like a ten-year-old Cuban guardian angel.

She stopped me at the door. "Oye, listen. We live in a nice, white neighborhood now. Can you fucking behave yourself? Don't bring home any drama."

I stood outside looking around like an idiot, not knowing where to go or what to do. I could make a right and go to the park, or I could turn left and head down Charles Court. I heard the sounds of what I thought were other kids playing, so I turned left and followed the noises.

There was a fight. It was one Italian kid named Anthony Balzano alone against a bunch of Irish kids, the Robson brothers. That shit wasn't fair. I immediately jumped in on the underdog's side and started throwing punches. I was scared, and we were outnumbered, but I didn't give a fuck. I was the guardian angel!

After Mr. Robson came and broke it up, he smacked Anthony and tossed him into the side of a car like it was nothing. Unfortunately for Mr. Robson, he didn't think that out too well. Anthony went in his friend's house to use the phone, and the Robsons walked back to their apartment. Within a few minutes, two cars raced up Charles Court, a regular cop car and a detective car, all black with a single red light on top.

The patrolman stayed put while the detective, Anthony's dad Carmine, hopped out of his car and walked straight toward us. Carmine was a stocky dude with hands each the size of a prosciutto ham. Carmine checked out the damage laid on his son, then walked up the Robson's apartment stairs, knocked on the door, and beat the living fuck out of Mr. Robson. A full-on scene from a movie. Blood everywhere. Guts everywhere (or so I like to remember it). It was fucking tremendous.

When he was finished, Carmine came back down and asked who I was.

"Name is Joey, we just moved here," I said.

"So you're the new spic on the block?" he laughed. "I appreciate you sticking up for my son."

Anthony and I hopped into his dad's detective car, and we pulled up in front of my house. I saw my mom on the porch sweeping, and the second she saw the cop car with me in the back, the anger washed over her face. When I got out of the car, my white outfit covered in dirt and gravel, her face reddened even more. She tipped the broom upside down and started unscrewing the handle, ready to lay a beating on me.

"Oh, Jose Antonio!" she yelled. "What did I tell you?"

Carmine rushed up to the house, his hands stained in Mr. Robson's blood.

"It's not what you think," he said, shaking his head. "Your son jumped into a fight to help my son. That's a good kid you have here."

"So he's not in trouble?" It was the only real thing my mom cared about in that moment.

"Not at all. I'd like to have him over to our house for dinner."

The Balzanos became my second family from that day forward, Anthony like my brother. I even eventually started calling his mother "Ma." I liked the way the Balzanos talked to me—like I was really one of their own. The Balzanos didn't care what background you came from; if you were in with their family, you were *in*. All of us neighborhood kids got to calling Carmine our "United Nations Dad" because he always had a mix of different nationalities at his house at any given time.

I ate dinner there that first night, and over the years, managed to eat many of my meals in that very house. Plus, the beauty of becoming close with the Balzanos as a new kid to the neighborhood was having Carmine's name to throw out whenever shit got too crazy.

"You don't want me to call my father, do you?" was one of Anthony's favorite lines. It worked every time. That's because no one, and I repeat *no one*, wanted to fuck with Carmine Balzano. Not only because he was a cop, but because he would destroy them with a simple crack to the head.

There was this one family on our block, the Clemens, and we would just rag on them all the time—constantly saying the family had lice and shit like that. Whatever we could say to piss them off, we said it. One day we were outside playing in the street, and Mr. Clemens came out and called Anthony a guinea. The second Carmine heard about this, it was on.

Carmine punched Mr. Clemens right in the fucking mouth, handcuffed him, and then beat him with his walkie-talkie. As Mr. Clemens was screaming, "Police brutality! Police brutality!" people were coming outside to see what was happening, then turning right back around and going inside like nothing. Mr. Clemens was covered in blood from head to toe, and not one person called the cops or got involved.

See what I mean? Fighting was the norm. With these kinds of influences, us kids took every opportunity to throw down, too. Even if it meant beating up a nun.

I went to Catholic school from third to fifth grade, and it didn't take very long there to realize the nuns were not women—they were something else entirely. They thought nothing of physically and mentally abusing every kid. If you went to Catholic school in the '70s, you know exactly what I'm talking about.

I went to Sacred Heart School for Boys in Kearny, and the biggest asshole nun there by far was Sister Hyacith. This woman didn't fuck around. She didn't necessarily get pissed at us for being bad kids. It was because we wouldn't drink our milk. What can I say? I didn't like milk. (Fifty years later, I still refuse to drink milk. It smells like dick.) It was nothing for this nun to crack me over the head with a lunch tray for skipping milk, and after a while I was getting pretty tired of it. The rage I had inside for her was unmatched.

One day I saw two classmates of mine—twin brothers—sitting around crying, so I asked them what was up.

"Our mom is having a baby right now, and Sister Hyacith won't let us call the hospital," one of the twins, Rafael, said.

"Not for nothing, but Jesus doesn't keep the lights on here. That's your parents' money. Just go call her." I didn't give a fuck.

Sister Hyacith overheard and told all three of us to go wait outside of the classroom. I knew we were in for a beating. She went after one of the twins first, smacked him around a bunch of times, and he went down. Then, she grabbed the next twin and fucked him up. He was out for the count.

When it was my turn, she started bitch-slapping me of all things. That was a beating *and* disrespect. Now I was really about to snap. Then she told me to get in the utility closet, which just so you know, is where kids went to die. That's where they killed you and then called your parents and told them, "Oh, I guess he must have died of pneumonia."

We got in the utility closet, and she was really going at it—she was using hands, feet, elbows, you name it. I tasted the blood in my mouth, and that was it. I decided to fight back. I knew that if I went for it, I'd have to *really* go for it, though. This was a grown adult, and I was just a kid still, maybe a hundred pounds max with a crucifix in my pocket. I reached out, grabbed her by the veil, and started banging her head.

"Don't you ever hit me again, you cocksucker," I screamed at her. I was going *off*. Before I knew it, I got her into a headlock.

She screamed, "You're going to hell! You're going to hell!"

I screamed back, "So are you! So are you!"

We were making a scene, and soon another kid jumped in, wanting a piece of the action.

"Fuck this bitch," he said, grabbing her arm and twisting it around her back. Now it was the two of us against her, and a crowd started growing.

When I heard some of the other kids starting to chant, "Coco! Coco! Coco!" I knew we needed to finish her. There wasn't any turning back.

We dragged her out to the hallway, and we were still beating on her when it came to me that we should call my mother. One of the kids dialed for me and put the phone to my ear.

"The nun hit me," I told my mom when she answered.

The school was about thirty minutes from my mother's bar, but that day she made it in eight. When she got there, she found the nun on the floor, veil pulled off, shoes off, hair everywhere, and my mom had no sympathy.

"You need to get fucked so you can have your own kids and beat them, you piece of shit," my mom screamed at her, dead serious.

When the fight calmed down, we all had to get together in the principal's office and of course the verdict was that I was getting kicked out.

"He's not going anywhere," my mom told them. "The only way I'm letting you kick him out is if you give me back the deposit I gave you when he started here . . . but it has to be in all five-dollar bills."

"Huh?" The principal was about as confused as could be. "We don't have five-dollar bills to give you right now."

"Then, he stays."

That's just what I did . . . I stayed, with no repercussions at all. I mean, that nun deserved to get her ass kicked, and my mother fully agreed.

4

Los Pájaros y Las Abejas

My mom was responsible for closing her bar every night, so she wouldn't get home until about 3 AM. Every morning when she'd get back, she'd wake me up, hand me some of the food she'd picked up for us after work—like a Cuban sandwich or fried plantains—and we'd talk about life. She'd have a few drinks in her, and more than a few lines of coke, but those early morning conversations bonded us tremendously.

During one of our morning chats when I was about six or seven years old, she forked over some advice.

"Listen, Jose Antonio," she said, "When you get older, you need to respect women and eat papaya."

I had no idea what she was talking about, but what she meant was that I needed to eat pussy. I knew nothing else about sex or the terminology at that time, except when my mother would have me tell the single moms to get out there and get some *pinga*—and the term "blow job," which I learned from a girl on the playground who said she'd give me one for fifty cents. I ran the fuck away from her and later asked my friends what this blow job thing was all about. When they told me, my head almost blew up.

"What do I gotta do to get a blow job from a real professional?" I asked myself once I knew what it meant.

My mom had this one sexy friend Tita who would babysit me from time to time, so I waited it out until the next time she came over. When it was just the two of us, I told Tita if she gave me a blow job, I'd give her a bag of change I'd been collecting that had about twenty bucks in it. When she agreed, I hopped in the shower, scrubbed my filthy little armpits, and put on my best clothes and a gold chain. Then Tita came in for the deed . . . and blew on my stomach.

"There you go," she said, grabbing my bag of change. "That's a blow job."

"That's not a blow job!" I told her. "Give me back my money!"

I complained to my mom the next day with little success.

"But she took my money," I said, "It's not fair."

"Why the fuck do you think Tita would suck your little dick for only twenty dollars?" she asked me. "Women in my bar *mama la pinga* for a hundred . . . and you think she would for just twenty?"

After we'd been in Jersey for a while, when I was around ten or eleven, I started learning a little more about sex from conversations with Puerto Rican Nelson, a dude in his early forties who lived a few streets over. He wasn't technically a pedophile . . . like, he didn't molest us or anything. He was just one of those guys who would walk around outside on the street in just a robe with no underwear, junk out all over the place, and he took a special liking to me and my preteen buddies.

Puerto Rican Nelson spent a lot of time with us—maybe *too much* time—throwing a football around or playing a game of basketball with us, but he made sure to keep his skimpy outfit the same no matter what we were up to. I can't begin to count the number of times I saw that guy's cock as a middle schooler. In exchange for the indecent exposure, we'd get him to buy us whatever we wanted when the ice cream truck came. Ice cream sandwiches, snow cones, and whatever the fuck else.

My first sex conversation with Puerto Rican Nelson happened one day when we were at his house. He was sitting on the edge of the couch, dick everywhere, nursing a hangover, and smelling like shit. We were trying to get him to come outside and hang out with us.

"You guys getting laid or what?" he randomly asked us, towel wrapped loosely around his waist.

Our answer was no, we weren't. Plus, no one had ever had these kinds of conversations with us, aside from when Arnardo, a local at my mom's bar who she had become friends with, would ask me, "You getting your dick sucked yet?" or "What's up kid—you pissing sweet or sour?"

"Well, I could get some women over here to suck your dicks if you want," Puerto Rican Nelson told us.

We didn't take him up on the offer. But we did decide to take him up on another one. We'd noticed he had a new girlfriend that just started to come around, and when he said he'd charge us a dollar apiece to watch them fuck, we happily paid the fee.

The night of the deed, we dressed in our little suits and tuxedos as if we were about to have sex, too. The eight of us smushed our heads together in a window around the back of Puerto Rican Nelson's house and waited. We didn't really know what to expect, but we saw and heard more than we could have bargained for. She was sucking his dick and then they were fucking doggie style, but it was when we heard her shouting, "Give me milk, Daddy!" that we nearly died. We ran the fuck out of there screaming bloody murder.

———

Now that we'd seen some sex, we thought we were ready to see more. Back in those days, if you wanted to watch porn, you had to order a reel-to-reel video in the mail, so that's what we did. My buddies and I put our money together—it cost $19.95 plus shipping and handling—and we waited six weeks for it to finally show up. They sent three videos and a projector to watch them with.

When the shipment came, we were pumped. We waited until my mom and Juan were gone, climbed up into my attic, put sheets up over the windows, plugged in the projector, and turned it on. It was just . . . horrible. Even though we didn't know anything different, it was still fucking disgusting. The two people were clearly all fucked-up on drugs; you could see the needle marks in the woman's arms. One of our friends was only about eight years old at the time, and when he saw the woman slather two pieces of bread in Miracle Whip, put them on the guy's dick, and start eating and sucking, he started crying hysterically.

It was something out of a nightmare. Luckily, we had Puerto Rican Nelson to run to and ask follow-up questions.

"You're not going to believe what we saw." We told him everything. "Is that normal?"

"Well, were they fucking in the ass at all?" he asked back. "That's what you're really going to want to do when you get a woman."

That set my expectations high, but I wanted to be realistic. I figured I'd start by getting a girlfriend and take it from there. Nikki was a girl I met in seventh grade, and something about her drove me crazy. I mean that literally. I couldn't stop thinking about her; I was obsessed. She was a cute, skinny Cuban girl who looked like Cher, with no tits.

My love for women started when I was a toddler running around with my mom's friends. But by the time I met Nikki, it took over my entire life.

It started out slow, though. She lived close to me on Charles Court, so I'd walk her to school and then home again. It went on like that for a while. Then, around Christmastime, she finally invited me inside. We spent the night watching *Donny & Marie*. Her grandmother sat right in between us the whole time.

Next, we started holding hands, and eventually we kissed, no tongue. By the time she started coming to my house after school, we were dry humping like crazy. That became our routine. We went to my house after school every day and dry humped to Earth, Wind & Fire albums until 5:30 PM, giving us just enough time for her to get out of there before my mom or Juan got home.

It was beautiful, let me tell you. Day by day I was falling in love with this girl, and nothing else in my life mattered. I stopped playing the sports I'd been into. I stopped hanging out with my friends. Looking back, everyone else probably found me to be very fucking annoying during this time.

It went on like this for a few months before one day my mom came home early and caught us mid-hump.

"What the fuck is this?" she screamed, chasing Nikki out of the house.

After a lot of pathetic pleading and whimpering on my part, my mom finally agreed to let us hang out at our house but only if she was home and only if the bedroom door was left open. Nikki and I would go into my room and pretend we were doing homework, and the second we'd hear my mom get on the phone downstairs, knowing she wasn't paying attention, we'd immediately start dry humping.

When Juan caught us without shirts on, things exploded again, and Nikki wasn't allowed over for two weeks. But, little addicts that we were, we'd play hooky from school in the afternoons when my parents definitely wouldn't be home.

We got caught again, though, and that was the final straw.

"Do you know your daughter is a fucking whore?" my mom told Nikki's mom. "An *absolute* fucking *whore*!"

After that, Nikki's family hated me because of the "fucking whore" comment, but I tried to hold on to hope. Nikki promised me we'd have sex at the end of the school year, so no matter how much hatred was happening between our families—I was sticking this one out.

But, the end of the year came, and suddenly Nikki changed her mind, about sex *and* about me. We broke up and I was devastated. I'd made my entire existence about this girl, and now she was gone.

There I was, thinking I knew so much about sex, only to find myself without it—and in a real shit situation at that. While I'd been caught up happily humping the school year away, my grades had completely gone to shit, and I found out I needed to do summer school if I stood a chance of moving on to the eighth grade that next year. But when I fucked up summer school, too, crying over Nikki, I officially had to redo seventh grade. I knew my mom would fucking lose her mind, so I vowed to never let her know I'd gotten left back, no matter what it took. (Like, I knew a girl whose father owned a print shop, and she would help me forge my report cards to say I was in the eighth grade. Then, the following year, I'd leave the house every morning and start walking towards the high school before looping back to the middle school, so my mom had no reason to question a thing.)

Meanwhile, I had learned one new, important thing about the birds and the bees: women have the power to take a motherfucker *down*.

5

A Double Life

For a while—starting when I was about twelve years old—Juan worked at a flower shop in West New York. The shop was owned by the bookmaker Juan worked for, a guy named Nico. Nico also owned another shop across town, so Juan would bounce back and forth between the two as a way of making a buck. Of course, though, there was more to the story.

What Juan really did was send a bunch of guys out with flowers every morning to stand on street corners in the Flower District in New York City. They would technically be out there selling roses for a buck a pop, but these guys were actually bookies, and people could place their numbers bets with them. Cops said nothing about it. Plus, if Juan ever got caught running numbers in New York, it would be a misdemeanor at worst. In Jersey, he'd be fucked, and, as I said, he wasn't the type to chance going back to jail.

Because I grew up watching people work their hustle like this at every opportunity, it came naturally to me when it was my turn to take a stab at it. Ironically, I really got my start by scamming Juan. Before working with Nico, Juan had been working in my mom's illegal book-making business. When he left her business for Nico—a bigger dog—my mom was fucking pissed. It drove a wedge between them that would only get bigger over time. I didn't pick up on it at first. But, always one to have her back, the more he started pissing her off, the more he was pissing me off, too. Then, I started noticing he was trying to put a divide between me and my mom, too, and it wasn't cool. Sometimes he would get my mom going about my grades, other times it was about who I was hanging out with and why. It was *always* something, though.

Our house in North Bergen had cash hidden *everywhere*, in front of and behind the walls. (And it was all filthy and fucking dirty, too.) By the time I was about fourteen years old, with Juan continuing to find shit to be mad about, he started accusing me of stealing his hidden cash from around the house. I was pissed because I hadn't taken a penny . . . yet. He'd constantly be screaming to my mother in Spanish something about me being a lying little bastard. When she'd come into my bedroom for our 3 AM chats, she'd press me on it.

"Are you taking money from Juan or what?" she'd ask, handing me a plate with a giant T-bone steak and potatoes.

"I didn't do it, I swear to you," I'd tell her over and over.

One day it dawned on me: If I was being accused either way, I might as well have a little fun. Juan knew exactly how much cash was hidden in every spot in the house. So I started to switch the dollar amounts in his piles, just to fuck with him. I'd take a few of the hundred dollar bills that were wrapped in aluminum foil in the freezer and swap them with some twenties from the pile under their bed. This little crisscross of bills would have him walking around the house scratching his head thinking he was going crazy.

Juan also had a huge jar of change that sat on a swivel in our living room. Every day when he'd get home, he'd empty his pockets of the change, random bills, and what he considered *precious* silver dollars that he'd have on him and throw them in there. I started emptying the thing out, day by day, watching the height of the change drop lower and waiting for him to react. It was the first time I'd actually taken money from him, and I was loving every second.

It took him a while, but he finally realized it was gone and he was screaming. That was fine by me. As violent as Juan was, he never put a hand on me, or my mother for that matter. And now I was a few hundred bucks richer *and* I successfully managed to piss him off. It was a win-win.

―――――――

While I was winning the war at home by scamming Juan, I started taking this hobby beyond the walls of our house and combined efforts with my buddies. We started with some little bullshit like dining and dashing and stealing the new Puerto Rican kid's stereo as his family was moving into the neighborhood. Then, we started scamming this dude selling comic books off his mom's front porch on 43rd Street in North Bergen. This guy had thousands of comic books, so he sealed off the front porch of the house whose basement he probably lived in and turned it into a storefront. He'd open up shop at 3 PM when everyone was getting out of school and kids would stop by to shop around, but my friends and I were looking to make a dollar or two off him instead. We would go up there, bust his balls asking him a ton of questions to get him distracted. While a couple of us were annoying him, the others would steal a few Batman comic books or some Silver Surfers. A week later, one of us would go back and see if he wanted to buy the stolen comic books from us.

"It's weird, what the hell," he'd say, confused out of his mind. "I was missing these, and all of a sudden you show up with them. Something's not right here."

He'd eventually pay up though, and then we'd be back to do it all over again.

Our crew kept our eyes peeled for other opportunities. Like, one night we saw a van parked on the side of the road with no one in it. We looked in and saw it was filled with tons of stickers, t-shirts, and iron-on patches. The next night, we saw it again, sitting alone in the same spot. After we saw it two more nights in a row, we decided that stuff was ours. We broke one of the windows, got the van open, and took every last thing. Then, we took it all and sold it at a festival in New York City.

The kids I ran with were also known to rob a train or two back then. We heard this rumor that Kawasaki sent their motorcycles through the Secaucus train station stop, so we started walking up there and hanging around the swampy area where the cargo trains passed through. When we realized the bikes really were there—and a bunch of other valuable shit—we went to work. We'd find the right train while it was stopped at the station, and one of us would break into a car and open the cargo door. The rest would wait on the side in the weeds of the swamp and, as the train started moving, whoever was in the car would push the boxes out.

Everyone on the sidelines would help carry the boxes away and hide them in the bushes. Then, we'd get someone who had a truck to come back with us the next day, load them up, and drive it all back to North Bergen. Sometimes we'd luck out and the boxes would have pieces to the bikes, and other times it would end up being something like a washing machine. We didn't care what it was—as long as we could sell it for a big profit and then split the money between us.

We never saw this as *crime* necessarily. It wasn't stealing; it was just hustling—like we'd seen our families do so many times—and this shit was fun for us.

At the same time, these buddies and I started messing around with drugs, too. We originally started fucking around with weed through Puerto Rican Nelson, who—in addition to teaching us about sex back then—had introduced us to weed, then continued to be our hookup for a while. He'd charge five bucks for seven joints, and we'd smoke them wherever our parents wouldn't catch us, load up on Visine and Binaca breath spray, and hit the roads in a fog. Sometimes, not even realizing what we were doing, we'd venture all the way to Times Square, stoned to the gills. A thousand things could have happened to a pack of young dudes roaming the tri-state area high as fuck, but we always made it back alive.

As we were about to hit high school, weed started to become more of a regular thing for us. I liked the way it made me feel. The anxiety I'd felt as a kid turned into total calmness when I was high. I felt like I could breathe.

———

I felt a lot of shame about using drugs at first. After seeing everything I'd seen when I was younger, I'd promised myself that I'd stay away from drugs altogether. Then, the summer heading into my freshman year of high school, we discovered acid, and that shit sent me into another dimension. I liked the acid . . . a lot. So I kept at it. If the weed calmed my anxiety, acid opened my eyes to be able to reflect on myself and my life. I was tripping balls for most of that summer—acid in the mix nearly every night.

A problem started to pop up, though, when I started to question what I liked more: running with these guys, pulling scams, and experimenting with drugs, or being an athlete.

Basketball had been my fucking sport; I played a damn good forward. I played in school—and any chance I could out of school. (I was that kid who was always riding his bike around the neighborhood with a basketball wedged between the handlebars.) People thought I could make it big, and so did I. I had a dream—like many little dudes do—of making it to the NBA. After I'd played in a few Five Star Basketball Camps with the best players in the tri-state area, I started to believe them.

I really liked my athlete buddies, the guys who kept it clean—including the basketball guys and the dudes I'd been doing karate with over the years. But between who I was with them and who I was with my crime/party friends, sometimes I felt like I was living a double life. Like, with my karate friends for example, I acted like a real goody two-shoes who was just interested in going to see kung fu films, going to Chinatown to buy Bruce Lee pictures, and beating each other up with nunchuks.

Right before my freshman year started, I decided to tone it down with the acid and get my act together to start prepping for basketball season. I joined long-distance running on the track team to get my endurance up, and I also perfected my jump shot and box-out defense. But when basketball season started, I was sitting the bench. I couldn't figure it out.

Listen, I was fucking around with my friends here and there, messing around a little bit with drugs, but I had also been working hard for years to be a star basketball player. Riding the bench rubbed me the wrong way. Especially when I found out the reason I wasn't playing had *nothing* to do with my behavior outside of school. Turned out . . . the coach didn't like me because I was fucking Spanish. (I didn't let my mom in on this in fear of what would happen. She would have cut his dick off.)

This cracked me. Basketball was my world, and now I wasn't playing because of this prick. (For years I thought about going back, finding him, and shooting him. He single-handedly killed a little boy's dream.) I ultimately decided, screw this, if he's going to bench me, I'm quitting. I told the coach to go fuck himself. My buddies and I resumed our typical hellraising. I still had one thing keeping me on the straight and narrow, though. One thing keeping me in that double life, and it was karate.

On my sixteenth birthday, I had a karate tournament. I made up my mind in advance that it would be my last one. There was a snowstorm that day, but I headed to the tournament anyway for my last go at it. Arnardo, my mom's friend from the bar, was at my house, and as I was heading out, he told me he would play my birthday number that day—219. As a birthday gift, if he won, he'd give me the cash.

I left the tournament with two trophies, and that was that. I told my karate coach, Kevin—a great guy who was a Vietnam vet and very disciplined and skilled at the sport—that I was officially done. Kevin and I had been practicing together since I moved to New Jersey. I hated to leave him, but a kid's gotta do what a kid's gotta do.

When I got home, I had another win on my hands. The number 219 had hit, and Arnardo stuck to his word and forked over my winnings of five thousand dollars. I'd never had that kind of money before. I gave a cut to my mom and used the rest to start my own bank account.

Now, I was cooking with gas. I had a guy out in East Stroudsburg, Pennsylvania, who would make acid (there are some crazy motherfuckers out in those hills!), so I started taking the bus out there, using my winnings to buy from him in bulk and bringing it back to do with my friends at whatever concert we were heading to next. Whether we were at the New Barbarians or Bad Company, we were always fully stocked with any drug we wanted. Then, my East Stroudsburg guy introduced me to THC crystal and angel dust, and not only was I doing that with my friends, I also started selling the shit back home, too.

For a long time, I refused to put anything up my nose. Cocaine was the drug I'd been around most growing up, and I wanted no part of it. But eventually I had a change of heart with that, too. I didn't realize it would be the beginning of a very long and tumultuous relationship with the drug.

And, there it was, my double life was officially over—and at the time, the path I chose felt like the right motherfucking one.

6

Bad Luck

Luck was always a factor in my mom's life, sometimes good, sometimes bad. I remember her superstitions as far back as I can remember my mother herself, and some were fucking comical. Like when I was a kid making my first Holy Communion. What should have been a nice, peaceful day turned into her stealing a church bell from the school because she wanted to take it to Mets games with her to bring them the luck of Jesus. For months after that, she lugged the bell in her purse to every game and would ring it like a son of a bitch from start to finish. She protected that bell with her life.

It seemed to be working, and the Mets made it all the way to the World Series that year. But, when they ended up losing the series to the A's, I found her in the living room chain-smoking and glaring at the thing.

"It's a bad luck bell, Jose Antonio," she told me. "Bring that hunk of shit back where we got it from."

The next season, she went back to sacrificing live chickens before the games instead.

It was rare that she'd let those bad luck feelings take over for very long, though—she was always on to the next thing. That was until a combination of work and relationship troubles took her down hard.

Let's start with the bar. At the bar, things worked a certain way. Cops were paid off to not talk about anything that was happening there. A friendly bribe, so to say. There were a couple of regular cops who would swing by every week or so, grab an envelope from my mom, and then the next time some shit went down there, they'd be the first ones on the scene to wipe the record of anything. That included the numbers business my mom mixed in with her bar business, but also drugs, stabbings, broken windows and fights, and anything that could have cost her the bar (or worse, gotten her jail time).

These two cops were actually nice guys. They weren't corrupt or anything like that, the way I saw it. They were family guys who'd just gotten used to taking a bribe for their extra hard work to help pay the bills.

That was how it was for a while, until one day I was at the bar and I saw this long-haired, dirty-looking motherfucker sitting there. Turned out, he was an undercover cop. Eventually, he and another undercover cop friend of his went up to my mom and told her they wanted money every week, too.

"We're going to put all of you fucking Cubans in jail if you don't give us our cut," he told her. "Your clock is ticking, starting now. Come up with the cash."

A week later, this douchebag came back again, and he started with her all over.

"We're going to get a piece of the action, whether you like it or not," he told her.

My mom, in typical form, stayed tough, and finally they left again.

Not long after that, my mom and I were over at her friend's house. This friend of hers was a Puerto Rican woman who also practiced Santeria, and once a month, this woman would pass a spirit. It was crazy to watch her do this: she would drink grain alcohol and spit it out all over the place, light all kinds of candles, her eyes would be rolling back in her head, and she'd be in a full trance while chanting some words I could never make out. Her kids and I would sit there and watch her in awe, giggling like little girls every time her head seemed to spin almost completely around.

That night, she was in the middle of one of her sessions when suddenly she went right over to my mom.

"What's been going on?" she asked her. "Has somebody been giving you a hard time?"

Before my mom could answer, her friend turned around and picked up a white dish. She lit one of her candles and circled it under the dish. She did this for a minute before she tossed the candle and held up the plate for my mom to see.

"Is this the guy who's been bothering you?" she asked my mom.

I think I actually pissed my pants when I looked at the plate and it had an image of that dickhead undercover cop on it. I swear to fucking God. She lifted the dish over her head and broke it. It smashed into a million pieces as she screamed, "Seven days!" and did a cutting motion across her neck with her thumb.

My mom and I didn't speak a word about it on the way home, but we both knew one thing: something was about to happen to this guy. A few days later after school I rode my bike up to the bar, and there were tons of Cubans in there doing coke and clanking glasses. It was a celebration.

I ran up to my mom. "What happened?"

"That cop . . . you're not going to believe it," she said. "He got shot last night. He's dead."

Turned out the dude had also been taking bribes from the owners of a local Cuban cab company that was far more known for speeding cocaine deliveries around the area than driving people anywhere. When he and his partner showed up there the night before with the same speech they'd been giving my mom, looking to collect, someone shot the fuck out of him; just straight up blasted him with a ton of bullets. His partner lived but never gave any Cuban businesses any more trouble (smart guy).

The heat was on at the bar from that point forward, and it felt like all of the Cuban joints were being watched extra closely. My mom's bar . . . it was watched *too* closely. Luckily for her, Juan always—and I mean *always*—had his eyes peeled for any chance she'd get caught with anything illegal happening at the bar.

He was at the bar pretty early one night—around 5:30 PM, which was out of character for him—and when I showed up, he asked me to do him a favor.

"Go outside and grab a hot dog from the food truck and look around at the cars," he told me. "Let me know if you see anything weird."

I came back in and told him there was on unmarked car sitting outside with two guys in it. Immediately Juan started moving. He had everyone in the bar hide their drugs and any evidence whatsoever that numbers were being taken there; he even had my mom hide the expensive jewelry she was wearing (she could have never afforded that jewelry as simply the owner of a local Cuban bar; it was a dead giveaway that money was coming from somewhere else).

He knew not to use a phone in this situation, so he and I left and we walked all over North Bergen—it must have been about eight miles of walking—stopping at bars like Club 38, Café de los Antitas, and El Brindi, to let them know in person to clean their joints up; the cops were coming to raid.

"Tonight is the night," Juan kept telling everyone.

Low and behold, we got back to my mom's bar around 10:30 PM, and we were in there no more than a few minutes before the cops came in to raid the place. Luckily for my mom, the only person who got arrested that night was the guy who decided to hide his aluminum foil full of coke underneath his wig. The cops caught onto his wacky hair right away, asked him to lift up the wig, and cuffed that stupid motherfucker.

———

No matter how much time passed, my mom couldn't seem to get past the fact that Juan had gone to work for Nico's numbers business. The way she saw it, she'd taken Juan in after prison and taught him the ins and outs of bookmaking, and instead of being her partner in her business, he took the skills he learned from her and brought them elsewhere. It was a slap in the face.

One night she and Juan got into one of their big fights, and my mom thought Juan flicked a cigarette at her. She waited until he was asleep, took a statue of a saint, and hit Juan in the head with it. It busted his head open, blood pouring out.

The next day, Juan packed his things, left, and never came back. That was that.

Usually when people break up they'll leave at least something behind—maybe a pair of underwear or something—just in case they want an excuse to come back. But not Juan . . . he took it all. Every last thing. That's how she knew it was really over.

Soon after Juan left, everything with the bar came to a head. One night, someone used the pay phone outside of the bar to make a drug deal. No one knew the phone was tapped until it was too late. The bar was raided again—this time without advance warning to hide things away—and it was shut down.

I was too busy being a teenager to realize my mom had a huge hole in her heart. It was sadness over the bar getting closed, and over Juan leaving, but it was also sadness that she'd been dealing with for years about my sister being stuck in Cuba. No matter what she did or how much money she'd thrown at legal fees, trying anything and everything she could to get her daughter out of Cuba, she hit roadblock after road-block, and it was eating away at her. Then, when a lady she knew accused my mom of cheating with her husband—a guy my mom was friends with and nothing more—it added even more stress to her life. Her drug and alcohol use, and her gambling, were all on the upswing.

With no bar to head to, she spent her days hitting the track—or any-where she could bet a number—digging us into a giant pit of debt. On a typical day, I'd have breakfast with her in the mornings, and then I'd be off to school, and she'd be off to the track and wouldn't be back until the wee hours. *Sometimes* she would come home for dinner, but I didn't fucking count on it. On most days, I came home from school to find a marinated steak and a twenty-dollar bill—I could either cook the steak for dinner or take the money and eat out. So I would cook the steak, pocket the cash, and meet up with a girl.

I was just minding my own business and doing my own thing. I was an independent kid at that age, financially and otherwise. I was doing my own laundry, making my own meals, cleaning up after myself; I was responsible for maintaining the house while my mom wasn't around. I was mostly staying out of trouble with her, but maybe she was too busy with her own shit then to even realize what I was up to day-in and day-out.

Attempting to stop the bleeding of our growing debt, my mom invested in a jewelry store because she loved jewelry. She ended up losing money in that too when the business went under, and back to the track she went. I later learned she also pawned most of her own jewelry—diamonds, gems, gold necklaces—and she forged Juan's signature to refinance our house. The only steady cash she brought in came from using our house as a holding station for drug dealers. They would store their weed and cocaine in our basement for a holding fee. But that income just wasn't enough.

In all aspects, she was holding on for dear life. She was desperate. Desperate enough to make a deal with the devil. His name was Tati.

Tati was a friend of my dad's and he stayed tight with my mom after my dad died. Tati was about six-four with a thin build, and he was dangerous. He was part of Alpha 66, an anti-Fidel Castro group (later recognized as a terrorist group), and violence was part of his being. I remember Tati and his wife, Nina, being around since, well, forever. Back during my early years in New York City, Tati would stop by and take me to grab some food or get a haircut, and he stayed around well into my teens, too. He was like a family member in a sense . . . except, unlike with other family members, I wasn't allowed in Tati's car very often because my mom was scared I'd accidently get caught in crossfire.

For the entire time I knew him, Tati was constantly in and out of jail, and because of this and many other reasons, he had a reputation. Nina used his jail time to her advantage; she had herself a little side piece. This dude was named Marcello, and he would step right in when Tati was shipped off to whatever jail he was heading to. Then Tati would come home and Marcello would disappear, until the cycle repeated itself. This went on for a while until Tati shot Marcello dead.

Like I said, Tati was dangerous.

Once my mom hit full desperation mode with her financial situation, she made a deal with Tati that came back to haunt us. By then, Tati was a wanted man. Men everywhere were looking to kill him, so he was constantly on the run, never staying anywhere for too long. He was looking to be "reborn" into the Santeria faith, but because of his shit reputation, he was having a hard time finding a place to do the ceremony. He needed to do it at someone's house, but people were turning him down one by one, because no one wanted to be involved with his bullshit. They didn't want that bad energy in their house.

"I'm looking for a safe place to do this," he told my mom, in her weakest state of mind. "But I haven't found the spot yet."

"You can do it at my house," she offered. "How much is it worth to you?"

Everyone we knew who practiced Santeria—including my godmother Beva—kept asking my mom if she was fucking crazy, but for the ten grand he offered her, she would not budge on her decision.

After Tati did the ceremony at our house, the house got dark to the core. Windows started breaking, pipes started bursting, the grass stopped growing—it was really fucking weird. Then, white mice started popping up. One day I opened the cabinet to get a couple of slices of Wonder Bread and a mouse came shooting out. Before we knew it, they took over the house; they were everywhere. I'm not talking about a few; I'm talking mice in every room and running through every wall. My mom's life was literally collapsing around her. And, if she had bad luck before, it was only going to get worse—this time for both of us.

7

Be a Man

Back in eighth grade I dated a girl named Colleen. She was a beautiful Irish girl who I met while I was playing on a Christian Youth Organization basketball team. She was a very innocent girl, and we'd get together on Saturdays to get a slice of pizza and walk down the Bergen line, me holding onto her alarmingly cold hands. We swapped spit all the time, but there was no sex. We'd just have our little dates and talk on the phone; it was just fun.

On a snow day that school year, she and I had been talking about maybe taking things to the next level, so she said, "Listen, there's no school tomorrow because of the snow, and no one will be home here . . . why don't you come over?"

So the next day I showered and put on my best cologne and my gold chain like a boss, and I rode my bike in the snow down to her place on 15th Street. I threw my bike on the side of her house and ran up to her room.

We put the music on, and things started heating up.

"What time does your family get home?" I asked her, praying we had time to get this party going.

"My dad gets home around five-thirty," she said. "Not sure about my brother."

"Oh, what about your mom?"

"My mom's dead."

In a second, whatever hard-on I had—literally *any* sexual thought—all went away. Her mother died? How could that be? How could God take away someone's mother?

"What do you mean?" I asked her, pulling away.

"Yeah, she died when I was five, but it's okay, my grandmother really jumped in and raised us," she said. "We're all really close now."

I was hearing what she was saying, but I couldn't wrap my head around it. All of a sudden, I was convinced I was going to puke. I booked it out of there and raced home. All I could think was, "What does a person have to do for their mother to die? What horrible thing must you have to do in your previous life for that to happen?"

It sucked, and I know it was really terrible of me, but I knew I couldn't talk to this girl anymore. It took me days to finally work up the nerve to tell her I was too busy with basketball and school to be dating her. She cried on the phone, and I felt horrible, but there was no way I could be around somebody all the time whose mother had died. It was the worst thing I could even imagine happening to someone. It spooked me out.

Fast-forward to the summer of 1979—when I was sixteen, heading into my sophomore year of high school. My mom was still mostly off doing her gambling thing all day, and I was keeping busy with my buddies. One brutally hot summer day—like in the nineties—a few of us went on a town bus trip to upstate New York, to this place that had these giant pools for us to go swimming. Standing in line there to get an ice cream, I passed out. When I came to, people were swarming me, asking if I was okay, but truthfully I didn't think much of it.

A few days later back in North Bergen, I randomly started spitting blood while running sprints in the neighborhood. Then, I spit blood again while playing basketball. School started, and when I spit blood a couple more times over the next few days—one of which was during gym class—my school nurse demanded I see a doctor. I went to our family doctor without telling my mother, got a test done, and went on with my life.

At the time, I had a nice little job at a place called J. Harm & Sons (it paid me eight bucks an hour when the minimum wage was something like three and a quarter—it was fucking tremendous). I was there after school and got a call on the work line.

"Let me tell you something, you son of a bitch! Why the fuck did you go to the doctor without telling me?" my mom was screaming. "The doctor just called and said you need to get rushed to the hospital."

Now I was screwed. She came and got me, and we went to Christ Hospital in Jersey City where I was admitted right away. I didn't get out for thirteen fucking days because they couldn't figure out what was wrong with me. We never got the full answer—some type of lung infection—but their best guess was that I'd accidentally smoked weed covered in paraquat, a toxic chemical. On my way out, I had clear instructions to take it easy for a month.

Hah! The night I got home, I did a hit of acid.

My mom convinced herself that me getting sick was her fault. She was making herself literally sick over it, too. Within a week of me being released, she went to the hospital for three days. She had ulcers and was diagnosed with diabetes. The doctors told her to quit drinking. Hah! That lasted about two days.

After our back-to-back hospital stays, though, something in my mom changed. We became closer than ever because, instead of spending her days gambling on this or that, she started spending her time at home. She continued to feel guilty over me getting sick—and that, combined with everything else that had been eating her alive—made her *different*, more present in every way. Our 3 AM chats were now happening all the time. She was cooking meals, hosting cookouts, and tuned in to my life. Sometimes a little *too* tuned in.

One Sunday, she was getting ready to have a cookout at our house for the Yankees vs. Mets game and asked me to make my bed before I left to go swim at the Balzanos' house.

"What the fuck am I going to make my bed for?" I asked her. "I'm going to go right back to sleep in it later."

Always quick with the comebacks, she goes, "So you're telling me, when you take a shit, and you know you're going to take another shit later . . . does that mean you don't wipe your ass? Make your fucking bed."

I still wouldn't do it and snuck out when she wasn't paying attention. I went to the pool thinking I was all slick, I was hanging out with my buddies and some cute girls, and suddenly I heard my name echoing through the streets.

"Jose Antonio! Jose Antonio!"

Before I knew it, there was my mom on the outside of the Balzanos' fence, whacking the top of it with a stick, screaming about my unmade bed.

"Do you know her?" one of the other kids said.

"I have no idea who she is, but she's crazy," I said back. "Call 911."

"Crazy?!" she screamed. "I'm going to kill you!"

I hopped out of the pool, unlatched the fence, and booked it. She chased me the block and a half home, trying to get me with the stick the whole way. When we made it back to the house, she said, "What the hell is wrong with you? All I ask is for you to make that bed."

"Well, I'm not making it," I continued to object.

She went to hit me with the stick again, and I blocked it with my arm.

"That's it!" Now she was really fuming. "You lifted a hand to me!"

She ran to the kitchen, took a roll of Bounty paper towels, and lit it on fire.

"I'm going to burn your fucking hand, you son of a bitch!"

She chased me around as pieces of burning paper towel fell on the carpet. As she quickly retraced her steps to stomp out the small fires all over the place, she spat out every Spanish curse under the sun. The whole roll was a giant ball of fire by the time she had to toss it out onto the front lawn.

———

She had a crazy way of showing it (sometimes *really* fucking crazy), but all my mom wanted was for me to be responsible. She had big dreams for me from the minute we moved to the United States. She had a vision of me joining the army, going to college, and then off to law school. She wanted her son to serve his country; in her eyes it was a form of repayment for letting us get out of Cuba and live here. (This is another reason she loved getting to every Mets game exactly on time—so she could stand proudly for the national anthem.)

Since she still had no clue I'd been left back in school and didn't think school was of any concern then, my mom also became strict about me calling to let her know if I was going to miss curfew. One night that fall, I was out with my friends and completely messed up on booze and drugs. I called her a few times to keep her updated on what I was doing.

After 3 AM, I stopped calling. I finally got to the door around 6 AM and the second my key hit the lock, she whipped the door open and went off.

"I was fucking scared!" she screamed. She smacked me right across the face.

Rather than argue with her in my fucked-up state of mind, I went right to my room, shut the door, and passed out. The next morning, she was there the second I opened my eyes with a glass of juice and a heartfelt apology.

"I'm so sorry, Jose Antonio," she said, hugging me as tightly as she could. She had tears running down her cheeks. "I've been going through such a tough time, and I shouldn't be taking that out on you. I'm going to get us through this. I'm just so tired lately from everything."

"It's okay," I said, hugging her back. "It's really fine."

"Jose Antonio, I just want you to grow up to be a man," she said, in a way that resonated with me more than it ever had.

The words, and *how* she said them, have replayed in my mind millions of times since then.

A few weeks later—in early November—we had Teacher's Convention week where we'd have a bunch of half days throughout the whole week. What it meant for students was one thing: party time. Every year, it's when all of the big bashes went down, and every drug was ready for our consumption. (It would have been the time frame for our annual Island of Insanity Party, too, one of our biggest of the year, but we always vowed to wait until the coldest night of the year for that one.) That year for Teacher's Convention week, we were ready to tear it the fuck up.

That Wednesday night, we had big plans . . . acid. First, we'd meet by Nick's Pizzeria, a place owned by a Greek dude who would pretend he was Italian. Then we'd head to a party and see where the night took us. My mom called me before I went out and said she wasn't feeling good and would be home early, which sounded fucking great to me. I figured if she got home around 1 AM, she'd be in bed asleep by the time I eventually got home. The last thing I wanted was her being awake and grilling me when I got back and sending me into a bad trip.

I met up with everyone, we did a hit of acid, and we went to the party. The cops quickly broke it up, though, and so I roamed the streets for a while, tripping balls. Finally, I decided to head home. I got home to find an empty house and thought, "Fuck!" I went up to my room, left the hallway light on (I'm scared of ghosts), and almost immediately went into an acid haze, in and out of sleep. I woke up a little while later to go to the bathroom and noticed the hallway light was off, so I knew my mom was home, but her bedroom door was open still, which meant she must have been downstairs.

"What the hell is she doing down there?" I asked myself.

I decided to go down and check, and as I got closer to the kitchen, I heard running water. I assumed she was washing dishes. When I got to the kitchen, I saw a vision that still haunts me: my mom lying on the ground unconscious, her entire shoulder colored purple. She'd had a heart attack.

I ran to her, checked her pulse, and felt nothing. I called 911 while my entire body went numb. I couldn't believe this was happening. I'd spoken to her just a few hours before. How could she be dead now? I checked her pulse again. Then, in that moment standing there alone with her dead body, a thought flashed in my head: "I knew she'd never find out I got left back in the seventh grade."

A joke? A joke was what came to my mind? What the fuck was wrong with me? It was not the first time, and not even close to the last time, that I'd make up jokes as means of coping with reality—that I'd try to deal with whatever negative shit was circling in my head using comedy.

I couldn't be inside with her lifeless body for another second, so I went outside and sat on the front stairs. I couldn't physically stand, my legs wouldn't hold me anymore. I was in total shock. Everything was moving in slow motion. She was only forty-eight years old; she was too young to die. And I was only sixteen; I was too young to be left completely alone. Who loses their mother at such a young age?

Colleen. Everything about Colleen and her family rushed into my head. I wanted to throw up. How was this really happening, I wanted to know.

———

I called Zoraida first. I still, 'til this day, have never heard a scream like hers.

The next day, my house filled almost instantly with my mom's friends—there to mourn her death but also to drink and do drugs. I loved Zoraida, my Uncle Lazaro, and Beva for showing up, but most of the people crowding my house were just fucking animals there to party on the worst day of my life. I hid upstairs in my room, imagining my mom walking in, turning on "L.A. Woman," handing me a plate of rice and beans, and telling me about her day like nothing happened.

But screams interrupted my brief escape from reality. All hell had broken loose downstairs when Juan showed up.

He and Zoraida were like a mongoose and a python . . . these fuckers did not belong in the same room. I can't remember much of their relationship before Juan and my mom broke up, but once he left, Juan was basically dead in Zoraida's eyes. The fucker broke her best friend's heart. The second they saw each other, everything erupted. I didn't have the energy for this, so I ran downstairs to set it straight.

"They don't want you here," I told Juan, pulling him over to the side of the living room. "It doesn't take a genius to realize that. I love you, but you have to go."

"I'm here to help you," he said. "How are you going to pay for the wake and funeral and everything else? I want to help."

I explained how an old friend of my dad's, a guy named Rivera who owned a local funeral home, had dropped by earlier. Rivera had shown up wearing a black suit and a white shirt, looking very formal to just be hanging around with the bums in my living room. While he didn't know me personally, he said he'd grown up with my dad in Cuba and that they'd been close until my dad moved to New York City. Fast-forward some years down the line, Rivera was living in New York City too, struggling to pay bills, busting his ass as a janitor and working other side jobs, and in a total financial rut. Out of nowhere, he was walking down Broadway and bumped into my father, who immediately gave him a big hug and asked how things were going.

"You know what he did?" Rivera had recalled to me. "He reached in his pocket and took out whatever he had and handed it to me. Then, he asked me for my address and showed up at my house with Christmas gifts for my kids."

"When I started my funeral business, I was putting money away to repay him—about a thousand," Rivera said. "Then, I heard he died, and I offered the money to your mom, but she wouldn't take it. It would be my honor now to have your mother's wake and funeral at my funeral home, free of charge."

Rivera's offer had given me a tiny sense of relief—at least one piece of this tragedy would work out okay for me. It was also tremendous to hear stories like this—things my parents did to support and help people they cared about. It helped paint a clearer picture of their characters when I'd hear things like Rivera's story.

As I was re-telling this story to Juan—explaining that I didn't need money for the funeral services—I was interrupted by more screaming in the house.

"What's in the fucking bag?" Zoraida said to one of my mom's friends who'd been bumming around the house.

"It's just a few things Denora said I could take if she ever died," the woman said, complete deer in the headlights expression. We all looked around at each other knowing damn well this wasn't true. My mom wouldn't even have a will in place because she didn't want to jinx herself into death. She never, ever talked about dying, so we knew this woman was full of shit.

Zoraida grabbed the bag and ripped it open. On top were some sheets and a blanket, but underneath was my mom's expensive mink coat.

"This woman just fucking died, and you're stealing shit out of her house, is that right?" Zoraida was furious, and honestly, so was I.

"Get the fuck out of my house," I said. "This is how you people mourn the fucking dead?"

8

A Cuban Farewell

One day after school when we were in eighth grade, Anthony Balzano and I were fucking around like usual, shooting the shit and playing basketball on the court across the street from where we lived (we were always kicking everyone's asses in basketball there—that kid could hoop.) At about 6 PM that night, his mom called us in for dinner. I had homework to do, though, and decided to eat dinner at my house that night. We said a quick goodbye and both headed our own ways.

The next day at school, Anthony was a no-show. Before class, I saw a bunch of the teachers gathered around all talking in serious tones, and I didn't think much of it until one of the teachers, Mr. Barone, came up to me.

"Did you see Anthony last night?" he asked me.

"Yeah, I was with him. Why?"

I knew before he could even get the words out that something bad happened. Mr. Barone explained that after they'd had dinner, Anthony, his brother, Frankie, and another guy named Steven took a ride to the supermarket. Frankie was driving, Steven was in the front seat, and Anthony was in the back . . . but he wasn't wearing a seatbelt. Someone ran a red light and smashed into their car, whacking Anthony's head hard enough to send him into a coma.

The condition Anthony experienced from the accident turned out to be rare, and the doctors struggled with how to bring him back. Anthony was in the coma for eleven days, and every minute of it, I was a mess. I couldn't concentrate on school, couldn't think of picking up a basketball to toss around—I was spaced the fuck out.

Finally, the doctors said there was nothing more they could do. They took Anthony off life support. He was only thirteen years old.

I'd lost my dad so early in life that my memories of him were limited. And while there was always this haunting emptiness I felt over my dad's death, losing someone who had become a part of me for years—like Anthony—hit me different. I didn't know how to cope, besides to stick close to the Balzano family and help fill a void for them where Anthony had been. I continued going over there for dinner and spending time with them as if nothing had changed. (I ended up staying close with Carmine until he passed away a few years ago.)

Anthony and I had been big Kiss fans, so at his funeral I buried my Kiss albums with him, vowing I wouldn't listen to Kiss again until I saw him next. I stuck to that promise until very recently, when I was having a tough day reminiscing about him. I can't imagine all the insane shit we would have gotten into together if we'd had more time.

I was just a kid when Anthony died, really, so I did the only thing I could to help myself: I blocked it out. I tried to focus on friends, and sports at the time, and kept myself busy. I was so busy that I hadn't even been seeing that my mom was going through hell; that she was deteriorating right before my eyes. Then, when she died, everything completely shattered, and I was alone. Like, completely alone. In a single night, I'd become an orphan.

The days following her death still feel surreal to me—especially her services. Sending a Cuban off to the next life is quite the motherfucking affair. At a regular wake, people are sitting around saying, "Oh, she was such a great person," or crying while whispering, "She'll be missed so much." Cuban wakes are a party. *Anything* goes.

These wakes are three days long, and the funeral home is open twenty-four hours a day. Inside, people aren't quietly mourning the deceased, like regular human beings. These fuckers are drinking, doing blasts of coke, gambling, you name it . . . all right there by the casket.

At my mom's wake, in one corner, people were slugging beers and gathered around a dominos board. In another corner, people were shit-faced and fist fighting. Frankly, I was embarrassed. On the first day, I'd put on my best suit and ridden to the funeral home with my Uncle Lazaro, my mom's brother who'd flown in from California. Zoraida, who'd quickly taken on the role as the unofficial boss of the services, was already there and had the funeral director by his throat. They'd put my mother in the wrong dress, and Zoraida was going wild.

"You better get downstairs and put the right clothes on her before I light this fucking place on fire," she yelled, tightening her chokehold on him.

As that brawl settled down, I started to see people showing up in packs of twenty. One caravan of Cubans rolled in the biggest fucking cooler I'd ever seen in my life, while each held a bottle of rum under their arm.

"Wait, wait, wait," someone working at the funeral home ran up to them. "You can't bring that stuff in here."

One of the Cuban dudes took a hundred-dollar bill out of his wallet and put it in the guy's top pocket, nodded at him, and kept walking in. Before I knew it, there had to be two hundred people partying in there, drinking and smoking cigarettes.

"What the fuck is this?" I thought to myself, before heading outside for a breath of fresh air. I soon realized this was probably what my mother would have wanted. She wouldn't have wanted people crying and shit— she would have wanted a party, and that's what she was getting.

For the three days, me, Uncle Lazaro, and Zoraida worked the wake in shifts, overlapping here and there. I worked 8 AM to 4 PM, Uncle Lazaro worked 4 PM to midnight, and then Zoraida took over until morning. My mom was never in the room alone the entire three days. The first day, a Friday, was balls to the wall. Saturday was balls to the wall, too. By Sunday, things started to slow down. That's when I was approached by Mr. Bender, a mild-mannered dad from the neighborhood who I loved.

"How have you been doing, Joey?" he asked, sitting next to me. "Do you need anything? Do you need money?"

"I'm okay," I told him. "I mean . . . I think I'm okay."

"Can I ask, who are you going to live with now?"

It hit me like a ton of bricks that I'd have to make a decision about this soon, like very soon. I shrugged my shoulders.

"Listen, it would break my heart if you didn't move in with us," he said. "You've always been a good kid. You and my kids are friends, you'll be right at home with us."

This short conversation with him made my fucking world; I appreciated his offer a lot.

"Thank you, Mr. Bender," I said. "I'll let you know what I decide."

Mr. Bender headed home, and the place started to clear out. The whole time, I hadn't broken down even once. I kept waiting for it, and waiting for it, but it wasn't happening. It wasn't until I was eventually left alone with my mother's body that I finally fell apart. The tears wouldn't stop. I must have sat there forever, tears pouring down my face, begging God for some kind of explanation. Finally, Uncle Lazaro pulled me outside and took me for a walk around the neighborhood to calm me down. When we got back inside the funeral home, I saw Zoraida in the room alone with my mom, kneeling at the casket talking to her.

"You're just so beautiful," she said, petting my mom's hair. "What am I going to do? You're a sister to me. How could you have left me like this?"

She was sobbing, "The world isn't going to be the same without you."

I stood there listening to her, realizing that what my mom and Zoraida had was the true definition of friendship. Even after my mom's death, Zoraida was proving to be a best friend, checking people throughout the wake who my mom didn't like or get along with, and quietly watching from the corner, doing a bump out of her bra every once in a while, all while making sure the wake was exactly what my mom would have wanted in every way.

"I'm going to make you a promise," she said at the casket. "I'm going to make sure your son grows up to be a man. I'm going to take care of him. I'm going to love him as much as you did."

Then, she did a bump right there at the casket.

"I'd offer you some, but . . ." she shrugged, and her tears turned to laughter.

9

This Can't Be Real

The day after the wake, we took the body from the funeral home to my mom's favorite church, Saint Joseph's in West New York, for the funeral. Then, we all went to Weehawken Cemetery in North Bergen. The cemetery was about sixty yards from where the Balzanos lived, and after we put the last flower on the casket and lowered it into the ground, I looked over to the cemetery gate closest to their house. The mom, Mary Anne Balzano, was standing there, and I saw her right arm was up leaning on someone . . . I swear it was Anthony. I walked up to her, and we hugged as we both mourned the loss of my mom, and remembered Anthony too.

Then came the exact moment I'd been dreading. All of the services were over and I had a giant "Now what?" hanging over my head. The good news was it seemed like everyone wanted to do good by me. The bad news was . . . well, my mom was fucking dead.

On the positive side, the sympathy sex was something I could get behind. Well, I was thankful for the thought behind it, at least. A girlfriend I dated the previous summer called me to come over and hang out. I figured it was definitely for a pity fuck, and I was down. We'd never had sex, but this seemed like a fine time for it. I went to her house and we were making out and things were getting hot. I pulled her pants down and it was steaming up even more, until I got to the underwear. A giant fucking brick pad came at me covered in blood. I almost fainted.

"Oh, my god," I yelled. "Pull your fucking pants back up. I can't see blood, it makes me sick."

"I just wanted to make your night better," she said, yanking her pants up, thank God. "I loved your mom. She was such a sweetheart."

I ran out of there as quick as I could. Truthfully, I'll never forgot that gesture though. I mean, anyone can give you a dozen flowers when your mom dies, but for a woman to offer you a mercy fuck when you just lost your mother, that's something you'll remember forever.

Meanwhile, people were flooding me with money to help me out—the many connections my mom had came out in droves, friends she'd made over time, family members I never knew much about—and I started stashing it away. I collected somewhere between ten and fifteen thousand from people donating to my cause: an orphaned sixteen-year-old whose parents helped a lot of people in their short lifetimes.

I knew I couldn't stay in my house alone, and it seemed like everyone wanted me to come live with them, in addition to Mr. Bender, which was fucking tremendous. As I saw it, I was now the number one draft pick. I had Juan or Zoraida, or I could move in with the Balzanos, or a couple of other families from the neighborhood like the Garcias or the Vilros. I could go stay with Beva up in the city, or even head out to California to stay with Uncle Lazaro.

I thoroughly weighed my decision, and all the while, I couldn't help but feel like the Benders' house would be the right choice. There was something about my brief conversation with Mr. Bender at the wake that stuck with me. Maybe it was his demeanor, or how he'd come up to me at what felt like the *right* time that day, but I couldn't shake the feeling that I was meant to live with him and his family. So I followed that instinct.

The plan became this: Zoraida would stay at my house with me for a couple of weeks as a transition, and then I'd move into the Benders' house that Thanksgiving. Those two weeks with Zoraida seemed to fly. Maybe it was because my brain still didn't seem to be functioning normally. Everything was one constant blur. When the two weeks was up, I packed some stuff into my suitcase and looked around at my room. Was it even *my* room anymore? It seemed like everything was taken from me all at once. We weren't sure what would happen with the house yet, so I'd still be able to come visit for the time being—but it would never be the same.

As I said goodbye to Zoraida, we made an important promise.

"I promise we'll talk every day," she told me. "And don't forget to meet me on Sunday at the cemetery."

She and I met at the cemetery that Sunday, and every Sunday for years after that, to visit my mom's gravesite together. And every week like clockwork, Zoraida would bring me two hundred bucks to help me out. She'd promised my mom she'd take care of me, and she was doing just that.

When Zoraida's cab pulled away, I walked with my suitcase over to the Benders, with no clue whatsoever what my future would be like.

When I got there, Mr. Bender showed me to the room I would be sharing with one of his sons, John. He showed me the dresser I would be using and my side of the closet. I went to the kitchen with them and—although I had been there a thousand times in my life—this time it felt very different. This dinner was special.

That first night sleeping there was a little rough. It was scary to be permanently gone from my house and my old life. I probably only got a couple of hours of sleep total. I remember staring up at the ceiling, wondering how I would really go on without my mom. I had to stay with another family *forever*?

A few days after I moved in with the Benders, Pink Floyd released their new album called *The Wall*. It was a highly anticipated album, so from the day it was released all the way through Christmas, everywhere I went this album was playing. There was no Springsteen playing, no Bon Jovi or Zeppelin. All you heard was this Pink Floyd album.

I liked it, of course, but there was one song called "Mother." I would be out with my friends doing mescaline or acid, and—it was inevitable—at one point in the night the song would come on. I would try with everything I had in me to keep it together while the song was playing, but I could sense that people around me would get uncomfortable and quiet. There was a giant elephant in the room.

The Benders only lived about a hundred yards from my house, so around the holidays that year I would walk by the house constantly and just look to see if there were any lights on, and I'd also walk down the hill to the cemetery and walk past my mom's gravesite. I thought maybe—just maybe—her gravesite wouldn't be there anymore; and then there would be a light on in the living room of my house and I'd see her walk by. I still had the keys to the house and some of my clothes were still there, so every couple of days I'd actually go inside, swap clothes out, maybe smell my mom's pillow, and then I'd head back to the Benders.

That first set of holidays without her was so hard, I can't put it in words. And throughout the entire holiday season, that Pink Floyd album was on; that song was on. And I was just crumbling into nothing. I knew I needed to mourn her, but I had no clue how to do it.

My mom's Cuban Christmas celebrations usually started on December 17, in honor of San Lazaro. When that day rolled around and it was *just another day*, it all started to feel *off*. The Benders did their best to make the holidays as great as possible for me, and I was so appreciative, but no amount of love, cookies, or gifts could fill that hole.

I'd gotten invites to a bunch of places for Christmas Eve night—Zoraida's, Juan's, and so on—but turned them all down. I wanted to spend some time alone during the day and then do Christmas Eve dinner with the Benders. Alone and wanting to keep my mind busy during the day, I headed to a strip club in North Bergen called the Meadowlands Inn. It seemed like the perfect place to distract myself. The doorman let me in without a problem, and I took a seat next to an old guy. I felt the weight of the world on my shoulders and hoped maybe this could help lift it.

But this strip club was fucking gross. These strippers weren't just dancing; they would do things like shove a Budweiser bottle up their pussy and then spray the beer back out at you. And, this particular day, it got nastier. The old guy next to me was holding a twenty, and the one stripper went up to him, took the money, and put it in her thong. Then she pulled her panties over, took out the guy's false teeth, and put them into her pussy. She took them back out and put them back in the guy's mouth.

Any thought in my head—good or bad—went completely away and I knew I needed to get the fuck out of there. The rest of that day and the next—Christmas Day—I couldn't wipe that image out of my head, which I guess was a lot better than having to miss my mom.

I woke up the day after Christmas thinking, "What was the fuss all about? I made it through fucking Christmas! Now I'm in the clear. My friends and I are going deep from now until New Year's. And I'm not worried about my mother anymore. Everything is going fine."

But then December 30th came, and all the negative feelings crept back in. There was a party that night at a girl's house on the other side of town, and there were maybe twenty-five people there—nothing crazy; people were really saving up for New Year's Eve the next night. By this point I'd started using drugs as a form of therapy instead of just for fun, causing me to have what I thought was the worst trip of my life watching *The Blob* with Steve McQueen. Thinking it could get no worse than that, I took two hits of mescaline. My friends and I were giggling and shit, and then out of nowhere I had this terrible feeling come over me.

It was anguish. It was pain at its finest. And almost instantly, "Mother" started playing. It was the first time I ever had a panic attack, and it was terrible. I put my beer down immediately and went outside to get some air, but the tears started coming and they wouldn't fucking stop. The pain was so intense that I puked, then I puked again. The alcohol was disappearing from my system, but the drugs were still very much there, and my mind was playing games.

Thinking back on that moment now, it still makes me very, very sad.

I started walking away from the party and I was crying more and more with every step. Without much logic, I headed to the cemetery. I jumped the fence to get to my mother's grave as quickly as I could, knelt down next to the tombstone and started digging with my bare hands. I dug and dug and cried. I couldn't believe she was gone. I wanted to know how this could have possibly happened to her. I wanted to know how this could have happened to *me*.

I knew I'd seen her dead on the floor in the kitchen. I knew I saw her body lying in the casket. I watched them bury her right there in the ground, but in that moment, I just couldn't believe any of it was real. It never happened. It must have been a joke. I loved God; he would have never done this to me.

"This is just a bad dream, and I'm going to prove it. Her body is not in here," I kept saying out loud to myself, digging until my hands were stained brown and my tears were frozen to my face. I laid on the ground next to the mess I'd made and cried more. I must have laid there in the freezing cold for thirty minutes before I finally got myself together to start moving again.

I jumped the fence the other way and walked back to my house. I sat down on the steps where I'd been that night and took a deep breath, and then I went up to the door and started ringing the doorbell. I had the key in my pocket, but I didn't want to open it myself. I rang the doorbell again and again. I wanted my mom to come to the door, open it and yell, "What the fuck are you doing?" I wanted to hang out with her and hear about her day while she shoved a coke rock up her nose and let it melt there.

I wanted to tell her I was there for her, that I was hearing her now, I knew how much financial trouble she was in, how sad she was. I wanted her to know I'd help her; I'd take extra jobs, whatever it took. I'd do anything to make her happy again . . . as long as we were together.

I wanted my life back; this certainly didn't feel like my life.

I wanted *her* life back.

Eventually, around 5 AM, I went back to the Benders' house and went to sleep for a while. When I woke up, I went to the cemetery so I could see in the daylight the damage I'd done to her gravesite. I fixed it as much as I could.

"I just want you to grow up to be a man," I could hear my mom's voice saying on repeat as I filled the hole back up with dirt. *"I just want you to grow up to be a man."*

PART 2

Criminal Life

10

The Devil's Student

My entire childhood was lived in full color; and they were vibrant colors at that. Even when some bullshit popped up, all in all I was a fairly good kid, having an excellent go at life. Out of nowhere, my late teens found me living in a black and white movie. It was a horror flick that never seemed to end. Everything constantly felt dark. I'd officially cracked from my mother's death, and there was no putting me back together. I was depressed, and the only way I thought I could combat it was by self-medicating with booze and drugs and lashing out at the world by committing an endless string of crimes. As I mentioned, my buddies and I never saw what we were up to—stealing stuff here and there—as criminal activity, we saw it as old-fashioned, fun hustling. After my mom died, that all changed for me.

I turned seventeen the February after my mom died, and that's about the time I started running with a dude we called "The Devil." He was two or three years older than me and a dark fucking guy. People warned me about him, but I'd stopped caring about my life at that point—and consequences for that matter—so from the way I saw it there was no real risk in hanging with him.

I liked The Devil a lot. He and I quickly got into stealing scrap metal and selling it for a profit. He'd end up shorting me every time—if my cut should have been a hundred bucks, he'd give me seventy-five—because he was the ultimate scam artist. I didn't mind. I mean, The Devil taught me how to get by on nothing. He opened my eyes to options I would have never seen before. I soon wanted to up my own ante.

With The Devil's guidance, I realized opportunities were constantly right under my nose. I took a job at a lumberyard every day after school from 2 to 5 PM, and part of my job was to bring the outgoing mail to the post office every afternoon. One day I got there and the post office was closed, so I started putting the mail into one of the mailboxes outside. An envelope fell on the ground, and when I went to pick it up, I felt something sliding in it. I needed to know what it was, so I put the letter in my pocket, mailed the rest of the shit, and got out of there.

When I got back to the Benders' that night, I opened up the envelope. Inside were two gas cards and two checks: one for twenty-eight thousand and the other for twenty thousand. Right away I sold the gas cards and then I went to a friend of mine to see what I could do about cashing these checks. He told me to call his brother, a guy in the mafia.

I met the guy at a local pizza spot and showed him the checks.

"What do you think?" I asked, showing off the smuggled slips of paper.

He examined them closely, front and back. "If my plan for this works, I'm going to keep the twenty-eight thousand, and I'll give you twenty," he told me. I agreed.

A couple of days later we met at the same pizza place. He gave me an envelope with twenty thousand cash in it. I was fucking set.

I never went back to the lumberyard. I used the money to start my own "business"—selling drugs, in bigger and better amounts than ever before. I'd go out to my guy in East Stroudsburg, stock up to the brim, and come back ready to sell a ton of mescaline, acid, and Black Beauties. My profit margins were fucking huge. Let's say I'd buy a thousand Black Beauties for forty bucks; I'd go home and sell them for a buck apiece. I was making money hand over fist.

While I was selling drugs in larger quantities, I was also doing them in even larger quantities. Cocaine was really blowing up at this point—*everyone* was doing it—and I used it to numb every fucking feeling of loss I didn't want to deal with. Beauty was, it worked. It wasn't long before my cocaine use was completely out of control. I went from doing it here and there, to doing it nearly every day. It was common to find me missing classes, high as fuck instead. Nothing seemed important to me—except having coke up my nose and someone else's cash in my pocket.

As the months passed, I became one of the biggest scumbags in the neighborhood. I'd gone from a kid fucking around with his buddies to a man to be avoided. Despite it, the Benders continued to be amazing to me. My reputation was going to shit, but they stuck by me. I was happy for it since I really felt like I had no one. So many of the people who'd shown up during my mom's services, who'd promised they'd be there for me for whatever I needed, whenever I needed it—now they'd disappeared; they weren't answering the phone.

Even my relationship with Juan was becoming nonexistent. He'd been pissing me off since my mom's death—talking shit about her to me, constantly telling me things I didn't need to know about her debts (we're talking hundreds of thousands of dollars), making her seem like a villain in her death—and I didn't fucking appreciate it. Then, my friends and I had a party at my old house and it was getting wild. Like, one kid was puking in the toilet, and I lifted his head up, took a shit in the toilet, and then put his head back in. Hah!

Juan showed up out of nowhere and reamed us the fuck out. He ended up changing the locks on the house and banning me from it. In retrospect, I can see where he was coming from, getting there to find all these kids fucked-up on drugs and trashing the house. But, back then, I wholeheartedly resented him for it. He was supposed to be on *my team*.

It made me even more thankful for the Benders, and really, how much they put up with. I think deep down they knew my issues weren't just related to my mom, or having to move, or having to give up my family dog, Crystal (she went to Nina, Tati's wife). It wasn't that my relationship with Juan had been severed, or that Anthony died, or even that during the summer my other close friend Dominick Speciale drowned to death. It was a combination of all of these things and more.

But the more I got into drugs and the more I got off on theft, the harder it was for me to stop. I kept acting up. Time went on, and cops were constantly banging on the Benders' door. It got old, and Mr. Bender finally had enough. He'd been patient for a year and a half, but in April of my junior year in high school, with tears in his eyes, Mr. Bender said, "I don't want to do this, but you're causing too many problems." He handed me a fistful of money and asked me to leave.

I thought I was going to be homeless for about a minute before a small bit of luck came my way. Another family from the neighborhood—the Runne family—told me I could stay with them. The Runne family had five kids, one girl named Joan and four boys: Mike, Steve, Ricky, and Bobby. I became close with all of them.

I contributed nothing to begin with. I was dealing a ton of drugs, bringing in a ton of cash. But what I learned then—and came to know very well for decades afterwards—was that when your life is mostly about partying, that money leaves your pocket as quickly as it lines it. So I was always broke.

By the end of that summer, Mr. Runne told me, "Listen, I have too many kids living in this house. I'm asking everyone to pitch in thirty-five dollars a week to help with the bills and groceries."

It wasn't a lot of money—and it was the least I could do—but I had a creepy feeling about using my drug income to pay Mr. Runne, if I could even hold onto it long enough. I figured I had a decision to make: go back to high school in the fall and keep scraping by like this, or quit school, get a real, full-time job, and pay my dues.

I had no family to impress, no one to walk down the stage and get a fucking diploma for. I had no one who would even come watch me graduate, I figured. No one counting on me to be a better person. No one counting on me for shit. So I said, fuck it. I'm done. When school started that year, I wasn't on the roster. It would have been my senior year.

I found a gig as a laborer at a warehouse. It was twelve-fifty an hour, which was great money at the time, so I started a thirty-day probation-ary period there right away and it was going tremendously. I liked it—so much that I was the first one there in the mornings and the last one to leave. I really started taking this job seriously. I even stopped doing coke on the weekdays so I could stay straight for my shifts, which was asking a lot of myself.

One day I ate something bad and started throwing up at work, vomit all over my jeans and shirt. I couldn't stop barfing. I asked one of the guys if I could take my break early to go to the Runnes' house and change, but by the time I got back, they had locked the gate outside of my job. I kept trying to call them to come back out and open it, but after a while without anyone even acknowledging me, I left. The next day I got a call saying I was fired. Apparently, I'd "walked off the job." I decided to fight it as unjust termination.

To bring in money immediately, I went on unemployment—and then, a miracle—my case against the warehouse went to the union. A few months after they'd wrongly fired me, I got about fifteen thousand in back pay. It was un-fucking-believable.

But in with money, out with money—so I was back to partying like a motherfucker and spending like crazy. Even though a lot of my friends were still in high school, we were going out every night of the week and you'd be surprised how quickly that cash burnt out. By spring I was back to illegal ways of bringing money in.

I thought to myself, "What would The Devil do?"

My first hit was the house across the street from the Runnes' house. The guy was a wealthy music executive, so I had scoped it out now and then thinking, "I have to get into this house." When I did, I brought one of my closest friends from the block, and we cleaned them the fuck out. Then, my buddies and I started mugging guys at night in Hudson County Park. I started regularly carrying a .32 pistol for protection, so I always felt prepared in case something went wrong. It never did. The dudes we'd mug in the park were little bitches. They would come there to get their dicks sucked—most of them married guys—and when they'd get there, we would be hiding in the bushes waiting to jump them and take everything they had on them. Since they didn't want to rat themselves out to their wives by filing police reports, they'd never say a fucking word.

My friends and I were becoming our own criminal enterprise. Every day was a different score. There was me, Stinky, Teddy, Carlos, Pelican, Jerry, and a few others who ran fucking hard.

There was a local jewelry store I noticed didn't have a security buzzer. There were always two old women behind the counter; they seemed like suckers. One day I went in and asked to look at a ring. One of the ladies took out a tray and put it on the counter. When she turned her back for a second, I took a couple of rings and put them in my sock. She never noticed a thing, and when I pawned them, I scored a few hundred bucks.

Not long after, we were all hanging out eating lunch one day and Teddy said, "Fuck, we need money for tonight. What are we going to do?"

"I have an idea," I said right away.

I walked over to the jewelry store and saw a case with what must have been more than two hundred gold chains—all different sizes—and underneath were a bunch of gold bracelets. I knew it would be a huge payout for us. Then, I saw what I really wanted: a tray of about thirty diamond wedding rings. The second the ladies weren't looking, I grabbed the tray, stuck it under my shirt, and booked it out of there. I brought it to a kid we knew, who bought all of the rings for ten thousand dollars. My friends and I partied like rock stars for a week.

That became our thing: steal something, get a giant chunk of change, party for as long as we could with the cash, and then repeat the cycle. None of us had jobs, but this was working out just fine.

One Monday Night Football game, my buddies and I placed a twenty thousand dollar bet that the Dallas Cowboys would beat the Pittsburgh Steelers. We bet through one of our high school teachers who was a really nice dude, so when we lost, we couldn't just dodge him. We had to come up with the money by that Thursday. We knew there were lots of places and people to rob, but we figured the jewelry store was our best bet.

I needed help this time, though, since word was out about recent robberies there. So we came up with a plan—Stinky was going to help me. I'd go in, ask for something, and when they turned their backs on whatever tray it would be, I'd pass it out to Stinky and he'd run out of there, then I'd run the other way. Stinky would pass the jewelry back to me at a meeting spot, and I'd hop in a car that Jerry would be waiting in, and we'd be off.

I had this weird feeling it was a suicide mission, but we went for it anyway. What did I have to lose?

The plan was moving along smoothly until Stinky dropped the jewelry tray as he was passing it back to me in the relay. The jewelry fell everywhere all over the ground as the women chased us screaming. We rushed to pick up every piece, and once we got it all, we both hopped a fence, got into Jerry's car, and sped away.

We saw a cop car speeding down the street with its lights on, but we stayed cool in the car, acting like nothing, like no big deal. When the trunk of Jerry's car randomly popped open while the cops were right near us, we were sure we were fucked, but for some reason the cop car drove right by us. We ended up making so much money off the jewelry— even *after* the bet was paid off—that we barely knew what to do with it.

After this robbery, people looked at us differently. They knew us savages weren't fucking around. I even got an offer to get involved with the mob after that—which was cool, but also terrible. I was making an even worse name for myself now.

Word continued to spread that I'd been involved in this big robbery, and another one of my former teachers, Mr. Dalton, let me know the cops were looking for me. They'd been to the high school asking around for information about me, showing my picture, and asking for someone who went by "Coco."

Coco used to be a term of endearment. Now it was the name of a criminal.

I skipped town for Sarasota, Florida, to stay with a buddy until things blew over. But it wasn't long before The Devil got ahold of me. He told me his sister-in-law's cousin was the owner of the jewelry store and that the heat was off. They stopped looking for me. Had they found me, I would have been locked up without bond and arraigned on a charge of robbery and for fencing stolen property. My hunch was the owner told the cops to stop looking for me. If they didn't arrest me, he could lie about the missing items and collect a huge insurance payout. My bet is he took the low road, but that might just be my low opinion of humanity. Almost immediately I got on a plane back to North Bergen.

My buddies and I went right back to fucking around. Like, on New Year's Eve—this was 1982—Pelican lost his fucking mind, got in a fight with another one of our friends, and the kid bit a chunk of Pelican's ear off. We had to drive him home holding a bag that had the piece of his ear it in, and I'm telling you, I've never puked that much. There was blood everywhere.

You'd think the jewelry store situation would have scared me into quitting crime for a regular life with an honest income, but you'd be really fucking wrong. Instead, I got involved in a big-time insurance scam run by this filthy dude named Zy. It seemed like everyone was involved in this: the hospitals, the lawyers, the doctors, and everyone in between. It blew my fucking mind. What you would do is get "injured" somewhere and go to the hospital with your fake injury. The hospital would recommend a series of doctors you needed to go to. You'd also, of course, get a lawyer involved to sue the location where you got injured.

You'd rack up bill after bill and, all along the way, you'd submit insurance claim after insurance claim. Everyone would falsely collect, all the way down the line.

When I headed to a fake chiropractor appointment the day Kim Duk-koo famously boxed Ray "Boom Boom" Mancini, everyone in the office was watching the fight. No one was really paying attention to anything besides the TV, so I snuck into a back office where a briefcase was sitting unattended, and I stole it. Inside were some checks and credit cards. I was able to cash a check without a problem by then, but when a shithead friend of mine tried to cash one I'd given him and got caught, he ratted me out.

I was arrested on January 20, 1983, for possession of stolen property—my very first arrest. I was taken to Bergen County Jail on twelve hundred dollars bail, and a friend's dad bailed me out. Instead of being overly upset about it, the guys and I laughed it off. How had I never been arrested until now? Joke was on the cops, really.

Eventually, I reconnected with a guy named Papo, an old family friend who offered me a gig running numbers for him up on 113th Street in Spanish Harlem. The job was seven days a week, which was good because it kept me busy and on my feet all day. It was honest work (even if it was illegal). I was making close to twelve hundred a week with him. It was fucking freezing—the middle of winter—but I was so happy to have a job again that I never complained.

I wasn't dumb, though. I knew this career wasn't going to last forever. I could tell the difference in volume in the numbers business now compared to my mom's in the '70s. In the years since then, the Pick 3 lottery had become popular and more ethnic groups started their own bookmaking operations, too. This business for the Cubans was on the downslide.

One day I got to the city, and they told me they weren't going to run the numbers that day. They handed me fifty bucks and told me to go home. It was only about 10 AM, and I started walking around aimlessly. I decided to go buy a bag of reefer, grab a *Daily News*, and maybe take the bus back to Jersey and get some sleep.

I walked into the weed spot and saw a really cute girl in there.

"Hi," I said to her. "How are you?"

"Hi," she smiled back. "I'm good. Hey . . . want to split a tray?"

"What's a tray?" I asked her.

"It's just dust that you sprinkle in your joint," she said back. "It's only three dollars."

"What the fuck, let's do it."

I bought the shit for us, and we walked to the nearby park and sat in the swings. She taught me how to roll the tray into the joint and then we smoked and sat there laughing for a long time. We started walking through Harlem and got to the end of Central Park, just circling around and enjoying each other's company. Before we knew it, we'd been walking around for seven fucking hours.

After a while, this girl goes, "Man . . . my baby is hungry," touching her belly. She opened her jacket, and she must have been at least six months pregnant.

"Holy fuck." I couldn't hold it back

"Did I just smoke angel dust with a pregnant girl?" I asked myself. I couldn't believe it. I felt so bad about it. I bought her a sandwich, some chips, and milk, and I got the fuck out of there.

For some reason, that was sticking with me. Of all the bad things I'd done since my mom died, I felt most shitty about that one. What would my mom think of me at this point, I had to wonder. Getting a pregnant girl fucked up on drugs? It was a very low low.

I knew my reputation had completely and totally gone to shit when, not long after that, my buddies and I were out at a bar and someone's purse got stolen. Everyone immediately assumed it was me. The weird part was, it really wasn't me who did it. I swear! They later found the purse—not in my possession—and everyone apologized, but it didn't matter. I was at the end of my rope. Something needed to change.

11

The Snowmass Village Thief

Jimmy Burkle was a guy from the neighborhood. I didn't know him personally, but I'd heard of him—a tough guy who was also very book smart. One night while posted up at the bar drinking my usual, a Southern Comfort and orange juice, Jimmy sat next to me and introduced himself.

"Yeah, I'm only in town for a couple of weeks," he explained. "Grabbing some stuff and bringing it back out to Colorado."

"You live out there now?" I asked.

"Yeah, in Basalt. Right by Aspen."

"How you liking it?" I was curious as fuck.

"I love it, man. Different from here for sure. Can't wait to get back."

The following night, he and I met up at the bar again.

"Do you think I could go out there with you?" I asked, almost pleading.

"Actually," he said, "you'd be doing me a favor if you did. I lost my license and can't drive, so I've been trying to find someone to drive me back."

I was fucking ecstatic. Jimmy was going to spend the next two weeks fixing up a crappy car he bought for seven hundred bucks while I got my shit together, too.

First order of business: I needed more money. I'd blown all of mine. My goal was to get four grand to bring out there with me. I decided to rob a bookmaker I knew who was notoriously careless with his money—plus he owed some money to my friends and had been refusing to pay it, so in my eyes he technically deserved it.

This dude lived in West New York, and I knew his property well—including the fact that he kept a vicious dog in his yard, exactly where I'd need to break in. Every day for a week, I went there to try to become the dog's friend. I'd bring a Burger King quarter pounder or a chicken sandwich and give it to the dog. I'd hop the fence to hang out with the dog inside the yard, and I even brought a ball to play with him one day. This dog was starting to like me, I figured.

The night of the robbery I got into the yard without a problem, and the dog was nowhere to be found, which should have made my job easier. But the second I started prying a window open with a screwdriver, I heard tires screeching in the near distance. I had no clue how they'd caught onto me, but it was the fucking cops.

They hopped out of the car and start chasing me, guns pointed. There were multiple fences I needed to jump to get out of there, and all of the commotion got the dog's attention, too; he came out of nowhere and started chasing me. I hit the last fence like a high hurdle and my first leg went over, but as my second leg was coming over the other side, my hand got caught in the barbed wire. I was wearing leather gloves like a true fucking thief, but the wire cut right through the glove and through my hand. The cops were shining flashlights on me, so despite the pain, I yanked my hand out and ran. I probably ran twelve blocks up and another five avenues over, all the while my hand gushed blood.

I somehow made it home, laid on my bed, and screamed, "Cocksucker!" at the top of my lungs. My money was gone. My big plan was fucked. Jimmy said, *Fuck the no license issue*, and ended up having to leave without me.

That Monday I headed to work at Papo's, and he told me there was a guy named Angel who'd been around looking for me.

"He's got a story he wants to tell you," Papo said.

I agreed to see him. Angel was a tiny Cuban gay guy, and nice as could be. He told me he hadn't seen my mother since 1969 on her wedding day to Juan, but he'd been friends with her and my dad and had tons of successful business ventures with them before my dad died.

"When your mother married that other man, she went against all of your father's wishes and started selling off those fucking investments," Angel told me. "The final straw was when I went to the wedding and I saw Juan wearing your father's jewelry. I told your mom it wasn't right, and she told me to go fuck myself."

We talked for a little while and finally Angel said, "You look like both of your parents so much. Do you have a picture of your father you can bring me tomorrow?"

I did, so I brought it to Angel the next day—and right on the spot, he handed me fifteen hundred dollars.

I stared at the wad of cash in my hand and was blown the fuck away.

"I loved your father dearly," he said. "No one in Cuba was okay with me being gay. They'd either beat me up or stop talking to me over it, and your father was the only one who stuck up for me. It meant the world to me.

"Because of that, I'm going to help you," he continued. "I want you to stick to your plan and go to Colorado and see what's out there, and I'll send you money every month. You got that? Live your life."

It was a miracle. An actual, real-life fucking miracle.

As if the stars weren't already aligning in my universe, when I crossed the bridge back to Jersey and went to the bar later that day—who was posted up on a stool? None other than Jimmy fucking Burkle.

"What are you doing here?" I asked. "You're back?"

"The car broke down in Pennsylvania," he told me. "I had to get it towed back here. It sucks. The car's getting fixed, and I'm leaving again in a few days."

If this wasn't a sign from God, I didn't know what was. I was a twenty-year-old dude with a bad name, but I was about to get a shot at a new, clean life.

It didn't take Jimmy and I long to drive out to Colorado, maybe a few days, and when we pulled up to Highland Hills—the condo complex I'd be living in with him—I couldn't believe my eyes. It was fucking beautiful. Everything around us was green. The air was unlike anything I'd ever breathed in Jersey.

Jimmy's brother had been living out there for a while so he had the place already set up. It was a four-bedroom house with a huge basement and living room and a patio area between all of the condos where the neighbors could hang out and grill. It all overlooked a gorgeous mountain backdrop. And it was dirt cheap.

I was loving life; I felt at peace in Colorado. I liked the laid-back vibe there, plus money wasn't an issue since Angel was lined up to regularly help me out. This was until I got a call from Zoraida after only a few weeks out there.

"Have you spoken to Papo? Did he tell you the news?" she asked.

"News? What do you mean?"

"Angel . . . he died of a heart attack."

I barely knew the man, but I cried the entire fucking day. In the short time I knew him, he made an impact. And frankly, I was also just tired of losing people.

To keep myself on the up and up, I decided to stay away from both coke and crime in Colorado and get myself a real job—one as a laborer at an asphalt company. I basically just pushed a wheelbarrow around all day. I even stuck with that job for a while until Jimmy and I decided to relocate to a place called Snowmass Village, about fifteen miles from where we had been living. It was in Snowmass Village that I committed my first robbery in Colorado.

It was like that brief time being drug- and crime-free—about four months total—all caught up to me at once and I couldn't help myself for another second. I'd been thoroughly addicted to both back in Jersey, and now the addictions were back in a flash. I started small, snagging a bag of cash out of the back office of a sandwich shop in the Snowmass Mall. I threw the bag in a dumpster behind a supermarket and hid the money outside of my apartment so I wouldn't technically get charged with possession if people came by looking for it.

That gave me the taste of blood. Now I had the bug.

I started robbing coke dealers almost immediately (and started doing coke again), stole cash from everyone else I could at any opportunity . . . I even managed to convince Jimmy to help me steal every last bit of furniture from a staged model apartment in a new condo complex nearby, including mattresses, towels, fucking wicker baskets, dishes, a table, a love seat, and so forth. It took us like eight trips to do it, and we did it all on foot because we didn't have a car. Picture us carrying stolen furniture down a giant hill and nobody said a damn thing.

From all my efforts, I managed to put away about ten grand, and I felt like I could rest on that.

Soon, drug dealers started to talk amongst themselves how they'd all been getting robbed, and everyone was suddenly on the lookout for who it could be. I kept a super low profile around those crowds—in fact, when coke would come out at a party, I'd lie and say I didn't do it, "never touched the shit," completely throwing them off. I was getting greedy out there, though. I started working as a dishwasher at a spot called The Tower Restaurant, and of course I'd steal food every night, but I mostly loved robbing the magician who worked the crowd there. He would ask someone in the restaurant to bet him one of their cash bills—in all sorts of quantities—that he couldn't use a thumbtack and a playing card to spin the bill into the air and stick it to the ceiling. If the money didn't stick, he'd give it back to them plus the amount they'd bet. If it did stick, he would leave it up there, stuck on the ceiling, and the money was considered his.

But the money became *mine*. He must have had like seven thousand bucks on that fucking ceiling because he would rarely take any down, so every night when no one was around I'd go up there and swipe a few bills. I ended up cleaning out one entire side of the ceiling before anyone even noticed. The poor motherfucker was fuming, but he didn't figure out it was me until years later.

The beginning of the end for me and my first go-around in Snowmass Village was Christmas Eve night. I went out and got shit-faced on Southern Comfort and orange juice and started walking around, breaking into three businesses and also stealing a safe from the construction house I'd been working in. The safe had just over a thousand dollars in it—no big deal—so I took the cash, threw the safe in a dumpster, and went home to bed, not thinking much else of it.

The next day there was a huge story in the Snowmass Village newspaper about a string of robberies the night before. Cops were on the hunt for the Snowmass Village Thief. No one suspected me, but I felt like I was cutting it close. And efforts to find "this guy" were heightened.

At the same time, one of my friends back in North Bergen had gotten stabbed, so I wanted to go home for a quick trip to see him. There was a jewelry store in Snowmass that I really wanted to knock off and hadn't gotten to yet, so I decided to do it before I left for my trip back to Jersey.

An electrician friend of mine explained to me exactly how to cut the wires of the store's alarm system, so my plan was to do that, then break the jewelry cases, take everything, and run out. I would leave a change of clothes at my construction house to throw anyone off who may have seen me, and then walk from there back to my place with the goods as if nothing happened.

Like a fucking idiot, I waited until the night of a blizzard to carry out this plan.

When I got to the store, there happened to be an extra alarm we hadn't accounted for. Sirens went off immediately, so before I could get any of the jewelry, I needed to hightail it out of there. I still went to the construction house as planned, changed my clothes, and went home.

About an hour later, there was a knock on my door.

"Have you been out tonight?" A cop was standing there, glaring at me when I cracked the door open. Another cop stood next to him, arms crossed over his chest.

"Oh no, I've been home all night," I said without hesitation. I peeked out around the doorframe, looked around, then shook my head in fake disbelief. "That weather is just *terrible* out there."

He looked down at my boots sitting next to the door, covered in snow.

"How come your shoes have snow on them?" he asked.

"Oh . . . well, I put them on to go get something out of the car," I lied.

The two cops exchanged a look. Jimmy was home and corroborated my story, but no matter how I sliced it, my secret was out. They finally had someone to start pointing a finger at, especially since the shoe prints in the snow showed my exact path around Snowmass that night.

Luckily they had nothing to arrest me for that night, but the timing was prime to get out of Snowmass for a couple of weeks like I'd planned. I got on the next plane back to Jersey. On the flight, I was sitting next to a soldier.

"Boy, I could go for a joint right now," he told me.

"Say no more," I said, grabbing a bowl and weed from my bag. In those days you could smoke cigarettes on the plane, but you sure as shit couldn't smoke weed. The pilot and the stewardesses went nuts trying to figure out where the smoke was coming from while we kept hiding the weed in between our seats, assuring them it wasn't us.

"If this continues, we're going to land and arrest everybody on the plane," the stewardess said over the speaker. The soldier and I just kept giggling.

Even in the little moments like this, the chaos never, ever stopped.

Back in Jersey, my buddies and I took full advantage of the growing cocaine epidemic, and when it came time to catch my flight back to Colorado, I couldn't bring myself to do it. I still loved Colorado, but I felt like I'd backed myself into a corner in Snowmass.

A couple of grams of coke up my nose, I made up my mind: I wasn't going back to Colorado. At least not for now.

12

Burning Bridges

Unsurprisingly, I'd only been back in Jersey for a few months before I was getting myself into shit—like getting caught stealing bottles of Dom Pérignon, every kind of vodka under the sun, and handles of rum from the bars I'd been working at. So when an opportunity presented itself, I decided to pursue another change of scenery as a means (or at least an attempt) to clean up my act and my name.

A close friend of my mom's, a guy named Rodolpho, got ahold of me and asked if I wanted to move to Miami to live with his family. Our families were close growing up and we'd spend every summer with Rodolpho's family when I was a kid. I jumped at the chance to go there. Rodolpho had just gotten out of jail, so I figured it was a good, clean house for me to be in and might help me change my ways.

On my second night there, Rodolpho said to me, "Do you remember a guy named Muneco? For some reason he wants to see you."

Rodolpho gave me a ride to Muneco's "furniture store" and when Muneco saw me, he hugged me right away and handed me a couple of hundred-dollar bills.

"Listen, I have a problem I need your help with," he said to me. "There's this rich woman up in Palisades who turned my son on to heroin. He overdosed and died. Can you talk to your Italian buddies for me?"

Muneco was convinced my mom had connections to get things taken care of. I guess all the years my mom spent talking to him about Carmine the cop, he'd gotten the wrong idea.

When I told him I didn't have a hookup like that, he started talking to me about drugs. He asked if I wanted to bring some coke he had back to Jersey, sell it for top dollar up there, and bring back the profits with a cut for me. Now *this* I could get behind.

So I started getting coke from Muneco for a low price, selling it in Jersey at high rates, and coming back to repeat the process. I did it about five times and made myself about ten grand per trip. On my sixth trip up to Jersey, I fucked up. I partied with my friends and did all the coke instead of selling any of it. This meant no money to pay Muneco when I got back.

Tail between my legs, I headed back to Miami. The minute I got back, Rodolpho's wife Vivian was standing at their front door waiting to talk to me.

"Don't think I'm a fucking idiot," she said. "It doesn't take a genius to know you're bringing coke back and forth to New Jersey. My fucking husband just got out of prison. I don't need this under my roof."

"I'm sorry. I made a mistake," I said. Immediately I knew I'd fucked this up for myself. "I won't do it again. You guys are like family to me, and this is the first time I've been around family since my mom died. I really need this."

"Pack your stuff," she said without hesitation. "You have to go."

I was crying, and she was crying, and Rodolpho was crying—but all of us understood deep down why I needed to leave. I felt terrible to have burned a bridge with these people who were so important to me.

While I'd fucked things up royally with Rodolpho's family, Muneco never said shit to me about the money I owed him. I went back to Jersey yet again, suitcase in hand. I knew trouble would find me if I moved back home officially, so I ended up calling my Uncle Lazaro soon after I got back to see if I could come out to California for a little while.

"Absolutely," he said. "Let's get you a plane ticket and then I'll get you a job out here, too. Maybe even something at my bar. This will be great for you, Joey."

I headed out to California in the fall of 1984. Uncle Lazaro was supposed to pick me up at LAX, but when I landed, he was nowhere to be found. I thought my mom and Uncle Lazaro had been thick as thieves. My mom loved him dearly, and they'd been the first to help each other whenever the other one needed it. When he left after my mom's funeral, he was fucking excited at the idea of me going to stay with him—then or any time in the future. So when he was a no-show to the airport and wasn't answering my calls from the pay phone there, I was unpleasantly surprised.

I waited at the airport for hours and finally decided to find a cab who would be willing to take the little amount of cash I had on me— something like forty bucks—for a ride to the bar Uncle Lazaro owned. I got dropped off and the bar was still locked up from the night before, so I just stood there waiting like a fucking idiot. I didn't even have a dollar left for breakfast.

It wasn't until about 4 PM that my uncle showed up.

"What happened?" I asked, totally confused.

"I'm not here to fucking take care of you," he said, pushing past me to open the place. "There's a bedroom above the bar where you can sleep for a few days and there's a shower up there—but don't plan on staying long-term. Get yourself a job right away."

I followed him into the bar, a blank look on my face.

"You know something," he added. "Your mother raised you wrong. And she was fucked up, too. Did you know after she died the FBI came to see me? They asked me all sorts of questions about her creepy fucking friends in that numbers operation she was running. I don't need this kind of shit in my life."

I'd never heard any of this, so I stood there speechless while he kept up his tirade for a few more minutes.

"So for years when she was sending you money to help you out, it wasn't a problem, but it's a problem now?" I finally snapped back. I was pissed. "And why did you wait so long to say any of this shit to me?"

Now I pushed past him. I found the stairs and went up to take a look at where I'd be sleeping. Right there on the bed was a fucking mouse. I was better off sleeping on the street.

Later that night Uncle Lazaro and I had another talk, posted up on two bar stools.

"I'm not giving you a dime for marijuana," he said. "I'm going to give you money for the essentials for a few days to get you on your feet."

He handed me a stack of newspapers.

"And, here, you can look at the ads to see where you can get work," he added.

"What about here?" I asked.

"Have you ever bartended before?"

"Yeah."

He thought about it for a second before responding, "Alright . . . let's see how you do on Wednesday. I'll give you a trial run."

For the few days I worked there, this guy threw jabs at me the entire time.

"You're a murderer by nature, it's in your genes," he said one night so everyone could hear. I focused on making the martini at hand as he continued. "Your mom murdered our sister's rapist; you're going to end up killing someone just like she did."

None of this made any sense. This wasn't the guy I'd always known. It didn't take long for me to lose my cool. I decided, fuck this douchebag, I'm going to start skimming money off the top here. I started hiding cash in my sock, my underwear, and in a crack I'd noticed in the wall behind the bar.

My next move was to get the fuck out of there—maybe head to Orange County or something, and bring the cash with me. I'd stolen about fourteen hundred dollars over those first few days, which would be enough to get me going. Now, I just needed out. After the bar closed one night, I crept around getting my stuff together and then went to grab the cash from the wall, but Uncle Lazaro was standing at the bar.

"You think I haven't been watching you, you little fuck?" He was furious. "Not only are you a fucking murderer, you're a fucking thief, too. Get the rest of your stuff right now and get out of here."

I started crying right away. I broke down. (You might now be able to see a pattern. I was a tough guy, but emotional, too.)

"I don't know why you had me come out here," I said. "This is not how you treat a nephew. You've been a dick to me since I got here."

Then, in a moment I'll never forget, he pulled out a gun and pointed it right at me. I pulled out mine and pointed it his way.

We stood there—guns drawn—in dead silence for what felt like forever.

"I knew you were a murderer," he finally said. "Pull the fucking trigger."

"I don't want to shoot you," I said. "I want to get out of here and never see you again."

I was angry, but I was so incredibly sad, too. The guns stayed pointed at each other until I backed out of the bar and into a cab. As the cab drove away, I felt like my insides were coming out of me.

"I'm truly alone," I kept thinking to myself. "Nobody wants me, not even my family."

I tried to use a credit card I'd stolen somewhere along the line to get back home, but it got flagged, so I had to use the stolen cash from Uncle Lazaro's bar. Now there I was, back in North Bergen, back to almost zero cash again, and nowhere to go. As much as they loved me, my friends were starting to slowly lose their patience, too—I was just a problem. People I'd ripped off, cops, and everyone in between were always looking for me, and my buddies were tired of constantly having to lie for me. A lot of them just wanted to move past that point in their lives, and there I was . . . stuck.

Soon after I got back from California, I ran into Gaby on the street.

"Where's your coat?" he asked. "It's the middle of winter, Jesus Christ."

"I don't have one," I told him. "I don't really have anything right now."

Gaby took me to buy a heavy jacket, but when he heard I was homeless, he couldn't be of much help.

"My wife doesn't want me having anyone stay in the house," he said. "But I have an idea of how you can make some quick cash so you can find your own place. I don't know if you do coke, but I have some I'm trying to sell, if you're interested in helping me out."

"Yeah . . . I don't do it, but my friends do," I lied. I was a fucking junkie, but what did he know? "I can definitely sell it for you."

I dealt coke for Gaby for about three weeks while I bounded around from couch to couch. Then on my last trip to see him, he gave me four ounces to sell, and instead of selling it, I did it all with my friends and never went back. It was all fine and well in my mind, until the day I was walking to get myself a sandwich from Hashway's Deli in North Bergen and I heard a motorcycle pulling up behind me. I turned around and it was Gaby.

"Where the fuck's my money, Joey?"

I started running—I didn't know what else to do. I ran behind a church, through a rose bush, which tore me up with thorns, and kept running until I got to the deli. I ordered my sandwich like normal and then three minutes later, Gaby opened the door, gun in hand, and started screaming. I ran to the back of the store where the owners' office was and begged them to call the cops. I wouldn't leave my hiding spot until the cops were there, I said.

When the cops came, they threw Gaby out of the store, but I figured it wouldn't be the last I'd see of him. He had it out for me now, and so did basically everyone else.

It felt like only a few people even cared if I existed. I remember the bartender at my regular bar, Joe & Mary's Tavern, looking at me with pure sympathy every time I was in there.

"I think my mom died of a broken heart," I said to her one day, gulping down my last sip of a beer. "Fuck it. Can I get a Southern Comfort and OJ?"

"Sure," she said, turning to make the drink, then talking back to me over her shoulder. "It could have been a broken heart, I could see that."

"She was really fucking sad all the time at the end," I said. "I'm not dwelling on it or anything but . . ."

I took the drink from her and slugged it back.

"You got a place to sleep tonight, Coco?" she asked. She'd gotten to know me well enough by then to understand I didn't.

"Yeah," I wiped my mouth with the back of my hand. "I'm all set."

I was far from set. That's when I started sleeping in the rocket ship in the park by my old house in North Bergen. When I wasn't sleeping there, I was crashing at different friends' houses in one big, ongoing rotation, sometimes inside on an extra bed or couch, sometimes outside on a lawn chair. I'd shower in that same rotation: sometimes inside one of the houses in the bathroom like a human, sometimes outside the house with a hose like a fucking animal.

I went mostly unnoticed everywhere I stayed, except whenever I was in line at the park with a bunch of kids waiting to get my morning drink of water from the fountain. If you think you can't get thoroughly ball-busted by a bunch of five-year-olds, guess again.

My days were spent posted up at the bar waiting for *assignments*. Sometimes someone needed to push an ounce of coke, or help load a truck, or sell some Quaaludes at the high school. I wasn't picky; I'd take any gig.

Aside from money and coke, I hated everything. If I saw a bug on the sidewalk, I'd step on it. If I was driving and saw a rabbit, I'd run it over. I wanted everything to die, like I was dying inside. Physically I was keeping myself fit; I had muscles and shit. But mentally, I was broken. Smashed into a million bits with no way to fix it.

I wasn't really sure what I had to live for; my life had no value. This felt especially true the morning I woke up on a mattress in the back room at a friend's house. I opened my eyes and saw a giant pile of dogshit four inches from my fucking face. I only really wanted to kill myself once in my life, and it was that day. I decided I'd do it by throwing myself over the George Washington Bridge. It seemed fairly simple to me . . . pop a few pills, pound a few drinks, and hop right over. In the end I just didn't have the nerve; figured I'd rather snort until I died instead.

During the holidays that year, a dude named Joel asked if I wanted to help him push coke, even though I had a horrible reputation for stealing from dealers. He agreed to have me help on a cash-first basis. The deal was he'd come to me with an eighth, I'd give him cash on the spot, I'd sell the coke, and then we'd do it all over again.

One night I was standing in front of the Midtown Lounge in the city and a car pulled up in front of me. The guy rolled down his window and it was my former teacher, Mr. Terranova, or "Mr. T." He was a really cool dude. He taught social studies, coached sports, and was an ex-junkie.

"What's up, man?" he asked me, looking me up and down. "Coco, you don't look good at all."

"I'm doing okay," I said, considering whether to tell him the truth or not.

"Well, you don't seem okay," he said. "Drugs?"

"You need something?" I asked.

"No, I mean . . . you using?"

I didn't know how much I should reveal to him, but I could tell by the look on his face that he knew the truth either way.

"Trying not to," I said.

Mr. T. parked the car and jumped out. He walked over and put his arm around me.

"You've been through some tough shit, kid," he said, taking a step back and examining me again. He shook his head. "I want to help you. Listen, I have a friend who runs a detox center. I can get you in. What do you say? You serious about getting clean?"

I was blown away at this. Mr. T. was doing me a solid here, and the way I saw it, if I wanted any shot at all of staying alive, I needed this.

"Let's do it," I said.

I took his number and told him I'd give him a call on New Year's Day. I still wanted a few days to party and make some cash—and I sure as shit didn't want to miss New Year's Eve for either of those causes. He was cool with that and said he'd pick me up wherever I was that day and get me to the detox center, no problem.

I knew Joel would be out on New Year's Eve night and would be relying on me to push most of our supply, so I took advantage of it. I told him I didn't have enough cash to pay up front this go-around, but if he gave me an extra ounce, I'd be sure to sell it all and make us both a big profit. I'd work the whole night for him. He must have not been thinking straight because he agreed.

He said he'd meet up with me on New Year's Day to grab the money. My plan was to be long gone by then. I sold about two thousand dollars' worth of the coke, did a bunch of what I had left, and crashed at a twenty-eight-dollar-per-night hotel. I woke up thinking I'd be out of there quick—able to dodge Joel without an issue—but when I looked out the window, there was at least a foot of snow that had accumulated overnight.

"Fuck," I said aloud to myself, hunting around for the hotel phone and dialing Mr. T.'s number.

"Mr. T., this snow sucks," I said and explained to him where exactly I was. "When do you think you can get to me?"

"I'm going to try to shovel my car out right now," he told me. "Give me like an hour and a half and I'll be there."

I hung up and touched my forehead. Burning fever. I felt physically sick and terrified as fuck that Joel would get to me first. I wasn't prepared to give that cocksucker a dime. I packed up my clothes, took some medicine, and stared out the window counting down the minutes until Mr. T. would be there, like a kid waiting for Old fucking Saint Nick.

About thirty minutes later, the phone rang. It was Joel. This was about to be a race against the clock.

"What's up, Coco?" he asked coolly. "I figured you be at that fleabag hotel. I'll be there to grab my money in an hour."

"Fuck," I screamed when I hung up. Now I was sweating my dick off.

All I could do was pray to God Mr. T. got there before Joel did. All I had in the world was one blue military duffle bag and I grabbed it off the floor and went down to the lobby to watch the parking lot from down there. Finally, I saw Mr. T.'s Cadillac rolling up. I ran to it, tossed my bag in, and told him to drive—and drive fast.

As we rolled out of the lot, I saw what I'd feared: Joel pulling in, dumb to the fact that I was in Mr. T.'s car making a clean getaway with a wad of his cash and his coke up my nose. I ducked my head down and told Mr. T. to keep driving.

A mile or so down the road, when we were safely out of Joel's sight, I broke down. I told Mr. T. everything I'd been through that year and how it seemed my life was over; like it wasn't worth living anymore but there was nothing I'd do to end it. I could barely breathe as I was releasing every emotion onto him.

"It's going to be okay, kid, I know it," he said. "You've been through hell, but you do have people who care about you and can help you, whether you want to believe it or not."

Years later, I realized that was true. I just couldn't bring myself to believe it in that moment.

We drove to Mr. T.'s house, and he made a few calls to find out the status of the bed at the detox center.

"What did they say?" I asked him when he was done. "Can I get in today?"

"Turns out the bed isn't open yet," he said. "But listen, we have an extra bedroom here. Why don't you stay with us for a night or two while we wait?"

I followed Mr. T. to the empty room. It was around 5 PM by then, and I got into bed and fell asleep right away. I slept until 11 AM the next day. Then I went back to sleep and repeated the cycle. I think I slept for the majority of the next four days.

After continuing to get a "nothing available" from the detox center, we decided I would stay at Mr. T.'s for a while and dry out. I ended up staying with him until about the end of February. Only a couple of people knew where I was, which was perfect; I basically disappeared into the wind. I was off coke and booze; the only thing I was touching was weed, which was nothing. The way I saw it, Mr. T. was really changing my life. It was one bridge I'd never burn.

Despite minding my own business at Mr. T.'s and trying to get my life together, my reputation in North Bergen was still following me. A buddy called me at Mr. T.'s one day. "Yo, Coco, did you do it? Joanne's house got robbed, and her mom thinks it was you."

It wasn't—I hadn't been in North Bergen in weeks—but that stung. I didn't really blame them much for the accusation, it *may* have made sense, but it was another sign for me that I needed to continue laying low.

Eventually I got a job in Mr. T.'s neighborhood at a liquor store, just trying to make ends meet. I started renting a room in a boarding house from a lady whose son would pop over every so often to smoke a joint with me. One night he had a gold chain on him and asked if I wanted to buy it. I bought it from him for forty bucks and took it over the bridge into the city to sell it for two hundred. Easy cash in my pocket.

Not long after, I was hanging out in my room listening to music on a stolen stereo, and the doorbell rang. It was the cops coming to arrest me for possession of stolen property. Turns out the fucking junkie son had stolen that chain from his mom. When they tracked it down in the city, fingers pointed back to me. The cops loaded me in the car while reminding me that I also had a warrant out for my arrest in Bergen County for possession of stolen tools for some shit I did a couple years back. I figured I was in for it.

The cop was a cool dude, though, and this lady's son was a known thief. On the ride to the jail, we stopped at a Chinese restaurant and had a nice meal together. We got to the station eventually, guts full of egg rolls, and I was put in front of the judge in minutes. All said and done, I was out by 11 PM with just a fine. When I was released, I realized I was out of a place to live; surely that woman didn't want me living back at her house. I called my buddy George, and he agreed to let me crash with him in Cliffside Park while I figured shit out.

I was able to save some cash quickly since I was doing most of my spending on stolen credit cards. I wanted to get enough money together to get the fuck out of New Jersey again and head back to Colorado, specifically Colorado Springs because it was the fastest-growing city in the country at the time. The timing seemed even more perfect when I got a call one day telling me an eighteen-thousand-dollar check was waiting for me from that old insurance scam I'd been involved with. I picked it up, cashed it, and planned to leave for Colorado immediately.

Two days later, I was all packed and waiting outside of a White Castle in Hudson County Park for a bus to Newark airport. I was standing there—my sole blue military bag next to me, along with a new bag filled with stolen merchandise—when I heard a motorcycle revving its engine.

"It couldn't be . . ." I thought to myself, looking around slowly.

But it was. Fucking Gaby pulled into the White Castle lot and stopped directly in front of me.

"You never gave me that money, Joey," he said, flipping up his face mask. "It's seven thousand, if your dumb ass is having trouble remembering."

"Shit, Gaby," I said, "I'm so fucking sorry, man. Listen I've had a lot of problems the past few months and I really am sorry, I mean . . ."

"If you don't bring me my money this week," he cut me off, "I'm going to shoot you dead."

I watched him screech away, shocked he hadn't realized I was leaving town considering I was waiting at a bus stop with two packed bags. Luckily, that was the last time I ever saw Gaby. Cocksucker.

13

The Cocaine Takeover

On a tip from a guy I met on a People Express flight to Colorado Springs, I rerouted my destination to Boulder. The dude thought I'd fit in better there. That's where I met Kathy.

Kathy looked like a female, white version of Prince. Her hair was cut short, like Jamie Lee Curtis, and she was blonde with blue eyes. She was sexy; she had a really cute little body, nice complexion, average height—maybe five-six—and gave off a skateboard chick kind of feel. She was a very sweet, innocent girl when we met.

Years later, I'd dream of killing her, but at that time—1985, at only twenty-two years old—I fell in love with her almost immediately. Or, at least, it felt like love. Kathy lived in the apartment right below me in Boulder. Even though she and her friends were always blasting music and I wanted to go down there and ask them to shut the fuck up, I never had the balls to.

When we finally did get to talking one day, we liked each other, and became inseparable. I was a loser heading nowhere, and back on my cocaine game, but she didn't seem to mind. Our relationship was centered on partying at the start—and she wasn't bothered by the person I was, even if that person was sort of a piece of shit.

Thankfully, considering my lack of cash, Kathy was a fucking superb cook—like, her buffalo wings were out of this world—and we ate at home a lot. When we did go out though, I was cool to spend on my stolen credit cards so she wouldn't suspect I had no money. She never asked a question about the cards. The Kathy I knew when we met was cool. No matter what I was up to, she was on board.

I got in the habit of expanding my wardrobe, including with expensive suits and shoes, by using the stolen credit cards at the Boulder local mall. Hanging around there so much, I ended up applying to work at the Foot Locker there. One day when I was working, a family came in carrying an envelope of cash. The second I spotted the envelope, I knew I needed to take it . . . so I did.

The cops were called and the blame quickly fell on me, but things escalated when the cops started talking about how I fit the profile of someone they were looking for who'd spent forty thousand dollars at stores around the mall using stolen credit cards. When they showed up at my apartment the next day to follow up, I knew I was fucked. Yet again, I needed to get the hell out of town.

Surprisingly, when I confessed the whole truth to Kathy, she was fine about it. Actually, she wanted to come with me, wherever I was going. We landed on San Francisco. I told her on a Sunday night, and the very next morning we hopped on a plane. We left without saying anything to her parents—just got the hell out of there. Kathy's parents were fuming when she finally called to fill them in, but we figured we'd worry about that whenever we moved back.

San Francisco didn't last long. After a whirlwind of my typical bullshit—swiping master keys from hotels to rob patrons' rooms, selling fake traveler's checks to San Francisco tourists, stealing bank deposit bags and cash from a safe during a job interview at an Italian restaurant, and so on—we fled San Francisco, too. I happened to talk to Jimmy Burkle, who was still in Snowmass Village, now house-sitting at what could only be described as a fucking mansion. He told us to come, so we did. The house really was *huge*—like a multimillion-dollar house, even back then. The living room alone was the size of most people's backyards.

We were only there a few days before Jimmy filled me in on some exciting news: he and his girlfriend were moving back to Jersey, and he wanted me to take over house-sitting for him. It was a dream. Kathy and I were only technically supposed to stay in the apartment over the garage—the house was off-limits—but who was going to tell *me* what to do, you feel me?

I started working as a security guard at the Crestwood Condominiums there, and Kathy landed a job as a waitress at one of the local restaurants. We were doing great as a couple—plus I stopped doing coke again, like *really* stopped—and we even got our own dog, a German Shepherd named Hercules. I wasn't even thinking about committing any crimes. I was so happy just having a girlfriend and a dog and living in this house—I felt so . . . *normal*. And whatever stupid shit I'd done before in Snowmass was forgiven and forgotten. People there seemed to have a short-term memory.

But, eventually, of course, I needed to complicate things. A few months into living there, a buddy from Jersey called me up.

"What are you paying for coke out there?" he asked me.

"Honestly, I haven't done the shit in over a year," I told him. "A couple of lines on New Year's Eve and that's it. But I'll ask around for you."

I found out people were paying eighteen hundred for an ounce, so I called him back a couple of days later and let him know.

"Can I come out to visit you tomorrow?" he asked. "I want to show you something."

He rolled up the next day with a bag of coke, shoving it my face.

"I could sell you this coke for eight hundred an ounce," he said. "And I can also teach you to cook it and recut it so that it still looks untouched. And you can double your money."

Sure as hell, I took the bait.

He left me six ounces, and I sold all of it in a couple of days. I also was back to snorting, too. Almost instantly, I was hooked again.

I started making regular trips back and forth from Snowmass to Jersey to run the deals. It started out great, as it always did. And it wasn't just the coke I was making a buck on shipping back and forth. One night I was watching *Miami Vice* and I realized—fuck it—I needed a new gun. I wanted the same shit Sonny Crockett was using. When I found out how easy it was to buy guns in Colorado, comparing to how hard it was in Jersey, I instantly saw a business opportunity: I was going to sell guns in Jersey.

Every time I flew back, I'd pack a suitcase with eight or nine guns and some bullets, top the suitcase off with some clothes, and I'd check my luggage without a problem . . . next stop, Newark. My friend would pick me up at the airport, drive us back to North Bergen, his mom would make us spaghetti and meatballs, and then I'd go sell the guns.

Later that summer, several months into our Snowmass Village stay, I got a call from some dude from the Snowmass neighborhood. He said I had a bunch of people who were pissed off. They felt like I was undercutting them with my coke deals and that I was disrupting things in their business. He demanded I meet up with them. I met them down at Snowmass Mall, and they asked me to get in the car with them. These motherfuckers had the balls to tell me to put a bag over my head while we were driving.

"We can't risk you seeing where we're going," the one guy said.

We drove for about thirty minutes, and when we finally stopped, they pulled me out of the car and walked me into a house where they finally took the bag off.

"Sorry about that, man. We weren't trying to intimidate you or anything," the guy said laughing. "Listen, we're part of something big here in the area and instead of us bumping heads, why don't we work together?"

At the time, I kid you not, I'd been able to put away about eighty grand in just a few months running my coke and guns back and forth. In the back of my head, I knew the money could disappear as quickly as it had appeared, as money had done in the past time and time again, but for now I was sitting pretty.

"What do you mean, work together?" I asked. "You guys are paying eighteen hundred an ounce. I can't pay that."

"We'll work with you on that, don't worry about it."

I told them I'd think about it; to just give me some time. Eventually I figured what the fuck . . . you throw spaghetti against the wall, eventually some is going to stick.

What these idiots didn't know though was that, while I started working with them, I was still making my Jersey trips. I was selling from both ends, staying in their good graces, and making a shit ton of money, storing my earnings in a shoebox under my bed.

I was told by these dudes to join the Snowmass Club, a very high-end golf club/spa and fitness center, and to do all of my drug deals for them down there. A bunch of people were in on it, including the receptionist at the gym. You'd hand her cash and go work out, then when you got back to your locker, the coke would be in there waiting for you. You'd take it, and sell it, and repeat the cycle.

The more coke I did and the less I slept, the more out of my mind I was becoming. I'd convinced myself I was the most badass drug dealer that ever existed . . . and I was acting like it. I started making these things called bazookas for myself. I'd take a coffee cup, fill it with three inches of water, put a gram of coke in it with 3/10 of a gram of baking soda. Then I'd toss it in the microwave for thirty seconds, pull it out, and take the chunks of coke out. I'd break up the chunks, put them into a joint or a cigarette, and smoke it.

If we ran out of reefer or cigarettes, our little crew—me and a couple of buddies out there—would use a bong to smoke it instead. We ended up smoking so much of the shit out of our bong that it actually melted. It was a party every fucking night. Our theme song at the time was "Hotel California," and to this day, I can't hear that song without getting some intense flashbacks.

Soon, I went from being convinced I was untouchable as a drug dealer to being absolutely sure I was being followed by the cops. I was sure I was about to get busted. I also started blowing through cash, which was going out of my pocket quicker than it was coming in. Eventually I stopped making the Jersey trips, and the money dried up right away. One day, I looked in that shoebox and there was no fucking money left. I had blown through it all with my bullshit and delusions of grandeur.

Cocaine goes from fun to scary quick. It seemed like one night we were all up on coke, talking and having a fucking blast, then the next night the coke flipped the card on me. My mind started playing tricks. I started to hallucinate all the time.

I thought every person I passed on the street was out to get me. I was sure cops were watching me everywhere I went. Before I knew it, I was spending most of my time looking over my shoulder at people who weren't there. I started hiding the coke and any little bit of money I had around in case I got raided. I also convinced myself that Juan was going to give me money, like half a million dollars of inheritance from my mom's death, and I'd leave to go to Europe or some shit. I was sure this money was, without a doubt, coming to me. This lie had lived in my head somewhere for years, but now the cocaine was making it seem even more believable. Needless to say, that money didn't exist.

———

There was one customer of mine who was a semi-regular, but I didn't like that he'd ask me to meet him at weird locations. I didn't fully trust this fuck.

"You don't always gotta hug me, guy," he said to me one night, shoving me off him. On God, I would never stop hugging him because I needed to make sure he didn't have a tape recorder on him.

Next time I met up with him, he wanted to do the deal at my house, specifically outside. This was a big red flag for me. I wore someone else's jacket, hat, and sneakers as a disguise, putting no thought into the fact that if someone was watching us, a dead giveaway would be that the deal was happening where *I* lived. When the customer got to me, I asked him to pull into my garage and I got in the car with him. I asked him to take a ride around the neighborhood as a cover. As we were circling back, at a house about ninety yards from mine up on a hill—there were cop cars. Then, I saw a guy sitting out there with a telescope. I knew they were watching me. Maybe these cops weren't going to get me that night, but they were definitely going to get me eventually. I fucking knew it.

I needed an exit strategy, and fast. Naturally, my only option to keep myself safe was to stack up some cash—by any means possible—and get out of Snowmass again. I did the math on where I was at, and

I'd gone from eighty grand up to owing a hundred thousand collectively to three different people. If I skipped town, those debts would surely be absolved.

By then, Kathy and I were sort of on the outs. She, too, was finally getting tired of my shit. The previous month she'd gone to Denver for her brother's wedding and I was supposed to fly out and meet her, but I got high and fucked it up. My flight was scheduled for Saturday morning, but that Friday night I scored a few ounces of coke, and it was *really* good coke. I did a line, then I did another line. One thing led to another, and I stayed up the entire night doing as much as I could with my buddies. I rescheduled my flight for later in the day that Saturday. By the time I missed my new flight time, I was *fucked*. My friends left and it was just me—peeking out windows, thinking people were outside looking for me. I decided to hide whatever was left of the coke in the sink so, in case the cops came, I'd run the garbage disposal and there'd be no issue; nothing for them to find except a maniac bugged out of his fucking mind.

I started roaming the house with my pistol in my hand, looking around every corner. I even refused to let Hercules outside because I didn't want to open any of the doors. Poor dog had to piss and shit in the hallway. By 11:30 PM on Saturday night, I thought I heard something inside the house, so I called the cops. When they got there, I could tell they were looking at me funny.

"Everything seems to be intact here, Mr. Diaz," they assured me, as I worried whether they'd check my sink, and if they were there to arrest me or protect me. "We didn't see anything of concern here . . ."

"I'm telling you guys, someone was here," I told them. They left unamused.

The next time I called them, not too much later that night, they brought a third cop with them and did a walk around the outside property, too. At this point, I was basically just calling the cops on myself.

"Listen," the new cop pulled me aside. "It's time to put that bag away. You're starting to see things."

"What are you talking about?" I asked, more paranoid.

"Sir, you're high. We know that. Try to get some sleep if you can, and don't call us again, got it? We're not going to respond anymore."

When they left, I noticed footprints near one of the locked closets in the house that I was *sure* weren't the cops' or mine. I decided to flush the rest of the coke. Whatever coke came back up from the swish of the flush, I licked off the bowl.

Despite me missing her brother's wedding, Kathy still loved me enough to ride it out for the time being. That next month was rocky, but when Thanksgiving came, my exit strategy was forced into play. I decided to have a Thanksgiving Day drug dealer party to get people on my good side, in case anyone was looking at me weird. I went to the supermarket and got a giant turkey and all of these custom steaks. I had no money, but I was acting like Johnny Bananas; I was making believe I was a fucking gangster.

I invited like eight people over, and all the food was set to cook that morning. But the night before the holiday, I bumped into an ounce of coke and got carried away. I didn't get back to the house until Friday. When I walked in, Kathy's face was pale.

"This can't continue, Joey," she said to me. Her tone wasn't angry at all. She spoke to me completely out of concern. "I think we need to leave."

"I don't want to stay either," I said, walking towards her for a hug. "Let's get out of here. Let's go back to Boulder."

We had eight dollars total between the two of us. I made a few calls to people out East and managed to get us about five thousand on loan. I had nothing to take with me to snort, though, which would be a problem, and I figured no one was going to give me anything in Snowmass.

Then, I remembered I had a pound of weed I bought that looked like something out of *High Times* magazine, but it was that Susquehanna weed—it did nothing to you. I wanted to get rid of the shit anyway.

"I have an idea," I thought to myself, after brainstorming for a while. "What if I try swapping this weed for some of Marina's coke?"

Marina was this badass chick who was heavily looped into the drug scene there. She hated me, but it was worth a try.

"I don't want to fucking hear it unless you have some of the money you already owe me," Marina said when I showed up at her house. "You got anything for me or what?"

"I don't . . . but wait, hear me out," I said, ready with a lie. "I have this customer who's stuck. It's someone we can't lose."

She stared at me, waiting for more information.

"Can you give me half an ounce of coke, I'll leave four hundred cash, and this pound of weed here for you, and then I'll bring you the rest of the money when I get it from him?"

Marina took the weed from me and sniffed it.

"Hold onto it so you know I'm good to pay you back," I assured her, hoping she'd buy in. "I'll bring the rest of the cash back to you and we'll be set."

What Marina didn't know was that I had my car packed—Kathy, Hercules, and all—and was ready to hightail it out of town the second I left her house. When she agreed to the deal, I took the coke and got the fuck out of there. Kathy and I got on the 82, pointed the car south, and we were off. I know we were still supposed to be housesitting, but I figured those owners would fare better with us long gone, plus that was the least of my worries.

"What's the problem?" Kathy asked about an hour into our drive. "The paranoia following you? I thought we were leaving that bullshit in Snowmass, Joey."

A young Coco dressed
to the nines.

My mom, Denora (left),
and dad, Manolo (middle).

A bunch of us got together at my mom's bar, El Reloj, in Union City,
New Jersey, to celebrate a birthday.

Me and my mom, fucking killing it.

Above: My eighth grade graduating class from McKinley School in North Bergen, New Jersey. I'm the dude on the bottom right. **Left:** Despite being left back in the seventh grade, I made it through eighth without a fucking problem.

NORTH BERGEN GRAMMAR S

Graduation Exercises

CLASS OF JUNE 1978

McKINLEY SCHOOL

CLASS MOTTO:

"To be, rather than to seem"

TUESDAY MORNING
JUNE 20th, 1978
at 10:30 A.M.

Graduates

Michael Allegretta
Louis Ricardo Arriola
Helen Avramidis
Rodolfo Gilberto Azcuy
David M. Bishop
Blanca A. Bolano
Osvaldo Bolano
Ralph M. Carey
Juan Carlos Carnicer
Nancy J. Clemens
Richard L. Columbo
Cynthia Lee Cotte
Claudia Alejandra Costa
Maria Elizabeth Curra
Carolina Cruz
Jeannette Diaz
Jose Anthony Diaz
Ramon Luis Diaz
Lillian Fernandez
Jose M. Fernandez
Grace Garcia
Marjorie Jean Giovanniello

Luis Hernandez
Paul Keltos
John J. Leach
Kathleen Patricia Leach
Nicolas T. Lescaille
C. J. McBreen
Lisa Margo Messina
Ana Maria Monroy
Miguel A. Montes
Miguel Novo
Addy Maria Ors
Anthony Lewis (Balzano) Patalano
Kimberly Ann Patterson
David Phillips
Bernard Patrick Robson
Carlos Sarduy
Louis E. Scarpati
Lucy Ann Schnorrbusch
Dominick F. Speciale
Jody Ann Stever
Jeanine Ann Tristano
John Steven Zanotti

Above: See, my name's right there . . . **Left:** Check me out, middle row at the far left.

Above: My childhood best friend, Anthony Balzano. Not a day goes by that I don't think of this kid.
Right: My other close friend from childhood, Dominick Speciale, who also passed away too soon. I miss you, buddy.

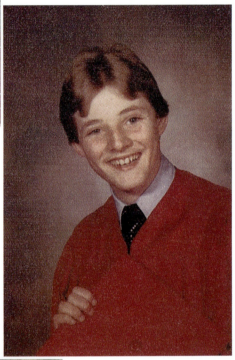

Carmine Balzano, the toughest motherfucker in North Bergen.

Hanging with a few of my buddies from the neighborhood. Savages!

Me and Mike Runne.

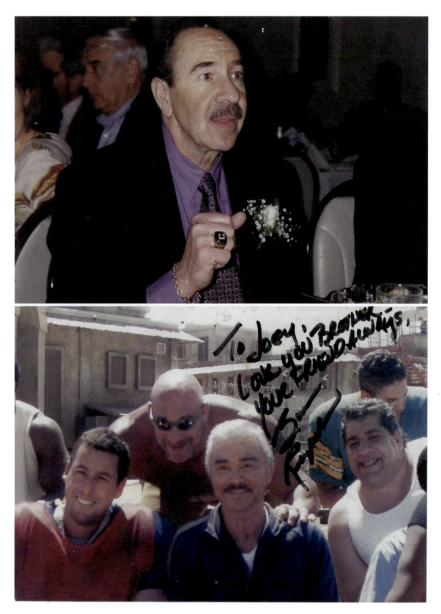

Top: Mr. Terranova, or "Mr. T." I'm forever grateful to this guy for helping save my life. **Bottom:** On the set of *The Longest Yard*, with a message from Burt Reynolds himself.

Above: Mr. and Mrs. Bender. My saving grace after my mother died. **Left:** Mr. and Mrs. Runne, who also took me in for a while.

Above: Mr. and Mrs. Ascolese. **Left:** Me with the Runne family.

"It's not paranoia." I was sure. "That fucking car has been following us since we got on the road."

Now both of us were paying attention. The car behind us stopped everywhere we stopped and turned everywhere we turned. This went on for another two hours. We eventually lost the car after a few quick turns, and I insisted we take the next exit and check into a hotel. We walked into the room, I did two lines of coke, and immediately I had to get the fuck out of there and go to a different hotel. People were watching us there.

"I mean, we're definitely being followed, right?" I asked Kathy on repeat.

We checked in and out of three more hotels that night before settling on a "safe" one. I did the rest of the coke there and didn't sleep a wink.

14

The Kidnapping

Beva read my cards one day before my first trip out to Boulder, and there were two main takeaways. The first was to stay away from cocaine (hah!). The second was to never, and she repeated *never*, do business in groups of three. I failed on that one, too.

When Kathy and I got to Boulder, she moved back in with her parents, and even though they didn't hate me (by the grace of God), I knew that wouldn't be an option for me. I got a place with a few other coke fiends, including my buddy George from Jersey. Next, I needed income.

A guy named Peter Pinto I knew from Jersey—who was now in Boulder, too—kept bugging me to come work with him as a car salesman for Subaru.

"I don't want to be a fucking punk," I told him.

"It's not a job for punks, Joey, you can make some serious cash," he told me. "If you come over, I'll train you and you can see if you like it. If not, you don't stay—easy as that."

I finally caved. I went down there on a Saturday to try it out. I ended up selling three cars that day and making a thousand bucks. I was a fucking natural. I joined the team, and that first month at the dealership was a dream: I was making great money, they gave me a car to drive, and being forced to wear a suit to work every day made me feel good about myself.

When it came to coke, my habit continued to skyrocket. The party was *on*. I went from partying two nights a week when I first got back to Boulder—maybe like Wednesday and Saturday—to three nights, and then four, and so on. Coke was everywhere in Boulder, including the dealership where I worked, and when I quit and went to the Chrysler store down the corner, I found out they did even more. Those guys got fucking lit.

I was a fucking mess. I'd get to the dealership early in the mornings just so I could rob the soda machine. I also knew the office's coke dealer never took his coke home with him, so in the mornings before he got there, I'd steal some of it and replace it with powder. When they realized I was a bad seed, I got kicked back to Subaru.

When the November 1987 stock market crash hit, people stopped buying cars. We went from making a ton of cash to basically nothing in no time. I had to keep my eyes peeled for any opportunity to bring in money.

And, just like that, it presented itself to me.

Kent Vella was a dude I worked with during my first stint at Subaru, and after we'd both quit then come back, we got to talking.

"You doing okay, Vella?" I asked him one morning at work. He had a black eye and looked like a pile of shit.

"Ehhh, things have been better," he said. "I got a DUI, so I don't have a license right now, which sucks. Hey, any chance you can give me a ride to the liquor store?"

As I was giving him a lift, he told me how he'd gotten shit-faced and crashed his car. When they took him to the hospital for minor injuries, he got out of his bed and went lurking around.

"Well, where you staying for the time being? You need a spot?" I asked.

"Nah, I'm staying with a buddy," he laughed. "That part's working out good. Always tons of coke around."

"Really?"

"He's been dealing for a while. Between us . . . fucking guy's got two kilos of coke that he's holding right now, just sitting in his room, but he needs to get rid of it quick. I'm figuring out a way to steal it soon, sell it, and move to Arizona. Figure then I can dodge jail and have money to get set up down there."

"You got any on you?" I asked, always with the coke front of mind.

"Yeah." He reached into his pocket and pulled out a baggie.

This was tremendous cocaine. It was beautiful. It was *perfect*. It was everything I could have ever wanted in cocaine, and more. I needed to profit off this situation, and I had an idea how.

"Hey," I said to him after a few lines next to the dumpster out back of the liquor store. "I have a dealer who will buy it from you when you get your hands on it."

"No shit," Vella said. "Alright, let's make it happen."

The second I got back to the work I called a buddy back in North Bergen.

"You're not going to believe this, but I found a guy we can take down," I told him. "It'll be a piece of fucking cake."

I was stupid, but I had balls of steel. I was chasing a lifestyle that didn't exist—and set on continuing that chase.

He agreed to give me some guidance—two heads were better than one—and told me I needed someone local to assist in person. I brainstormed for a while and then it came to me: Steve Tidwell. I'd worked with Steve a while back, and he was also my weed dealer. When he sold you drugs, he had to make it like a James Bond movie every time . . . he was a fucking moron.

Next time I saw Steve for our regular weed handoff, I let him in on my plan to get those kilos of coke.

"This is actually perfect timing. I really need the money," he said. "I've been hanging out a lot at this strip club, you know, having fun, and I met this girl. It's all nude there or whatever, but she's a really good girl. And she's beautiful."

I looked back at him, knowing this was going somewhere fucking stupid.

"Mm-hmm . . ." I responded.

"So the thing is, I fucking love her," he continued. "I really love her. And she loves me too. She moved in with me, if you can believe it."

I couldn't.

"The only problem is she won't sleep with me until she gets divorced. She's Catholic, and she takes that really seriously."

He went on to tell me how she took over his bedroom while he took the couch every night. She'd lock his bedroom door on him, but he didn't mind any of this. He stopped and waited for my response, but I had none.

"Anyway, the divorce is gonna cost her ten thousand. So I need to help her out. I need cash fast. Then she and I can finally be together."

"Yeah, makes sense," I said. It—of course—didn't. But what the hell did I care. This guy was clearly a little disturbed, but as long as he had a strong urge for this money too, so be it.

"My mom has a house that's vacant right now that she's trying to sell—what about if we use that?" Steve said to me over the phone a couple of days later. We'd been trying to lock down a location to scam Vella, away from his apartment.

"Works for me," I said. "When you thinking?"

"What about Tuesday?"

I'd been getting pressure from Vella—he wanted to steal and sell the coke right away so he could get the fuck out of Colorado. Once Steve and I figured out our end, I made the arrangements with Vella. Here's what we planned: Vella had a funeral that day, so I was going to stop at his place afterwards to pick him up. I'd bring him to the vacant house, where Steve would pose as the drug dealer. But instead of paying him, he would take out a gun and rob both of us, handcuff us, and take Vella's keys to go grab the coke. Then, he'd come back and let me loose and put Vella on a bus to Arizona so he'd be out of everyone's hair.

It was a straightforward plan. All Steve had to do was follow it.

When I stopped by Vella's to pick him up, I went into the apartment so I could scope out exactly where the coke was. He asked if I wanted to do a blast, so we went to a bedroom and he took out a grinder. There was about maybe half an ounce in the grinder, and we did a couple lines from that. Then he showed me a loose ounce in a desk drawer, and cash in the drawer, too—like one or two thousand dollars or so.

"Nice," I said. "Where are the kilos?"

"Up here," he said pointing to the ceiling. He propped open the tile in the suspended ceiling to show me. "We can come back and get it—let's just take a sample for now."

We took the sample and headed over to see Steve. I coolly made the introductions: "Steve, this is Kent. Kent, this is Steve . . ."

"Nice to meet you, man," Vella said, reaching out his hand. "You know I got these couple of kilos I'm trying to sell. I'm willing to cut you a deal. Say, twenty-five grand total. That's ten grand lower than asking price."

This is the moment I realized Steve must have watched too many episodes of *Miami Vice*. He didn't say anything in return, did a line of the coke, put the bag into his pocket, and pulled out a gun. He pointed the handgun to Vella's head and reached into his other pocket to grab a second gun . . . which he handed to me.

I stared at him—shocked out of my mind—thinking, "You fucking dumbass. You just fucked the both of us."

I was still processing what was happening as Steve handcuffed Vella and we dragged him into the spare room before putting a gag in his mouth. Even though I was confused about how this had turned so fast, my criminal mind knew not to let Steve rip me off either.

"You stay here with him, and I'll go get the coke," he said to me. "Where is it?"

"He said it would be in the desk drawer," I lied. "Check there."

This is what I get for doing business in a group of three, I thought to myself. Beva fucking warned me. Twenty minutes later Steve came back, now carrying a little machine gun.

"I found a couple of grams and like two hundred in the desk drawer," he said. At this point, knowing what I'd seen in that drawer, I knew Steve was trying to rip me off, too. "I looked everywhere for the kilos, and they're not there."

"You're a dumb fuck Steve—look what you fucking got me involved in." I was pissed that Steve managed to screw up something that should have, in theory, been pretty straightforward. "I'm out of here." I tossed him his gun.

I wasn't scared he'd shoot me or anything like that. This guy was stupid but not stupid enough to pull the trigger. I had my own gun in my trunk, and I had a vision of grabbing it and going back in there to shoot Steve dead. Then, I'd free Vella, and we'd be done. I wasn't stupid enough for that, either.

Instead, I jogged to my car, hopped in, and went back to Vella's place. I walked right past the doorman, opened the lobby door, and pressed the elevator button up. I got to Vella's apartment and kicked the door down like a fucking gorilla. Inside, I grabbed onto a chunk of the paneled ceiling and pulled down with everything I had. I pulled a whole section of the fucking ceiling down, and right there, wrapped in Colombian newspapers, all tightly sealed, were two kilos of cocaine.

I found a garbage bag to hide it in and got out of there as fast as I could. As I was pulling away, I figured for sure the cops were already on their way to find me, so when I saw a newspaper box, I knew what to do. Back then, it was common for dealers to hide drugs and money in the bottom of newspaper boxes on sidewalks—those boxes you put change in to take a newspaper. It was especially common for cocaine buys. I opened the bottom of this one and put the kilos in there. I'll never forget the newspaper box was across the street from a halfway house.

I raced home and called a friend of mine to let him know where I'd stashed the coke so he could help me get rid of it for a cut, which he happily agreed. I'd end up making eighteen thousand bucks from that theft.

Meanwhile, it was only about 3 PM, and it was starting to set in that I was fucked. When George got home, I told him what happened. Neither of us could figure out what I should do. I kept myself busy cleaning out the entire house, getting rid of anything that might incriminate me in any way: scales, rolling paper, that type of shit. We made dinner and . . . waited.

At around 7:30 PM, there was a knock on the door. George and I looked at each other like deer in headlights.

"Let me in," I heard Steve's voice outside. This motherfucking guy.

"What do you want?" I cracked the door open but wouldn't let him in.

"Listen, what happened today was a misunderstanding. I don't know what was happening or why I did it, but now I'm fucked. I got this kid in the trunk of my car . . ."

"He's in your trunk?" I asked, shocked.

"Yeah, and I need to drop him back off at the bus station—get him to Arizona—but listen there's another guy we can rob," he continued.

"What the fuck are you talking about?"

"She needs the divorce money by tonight!" he was screaming now. "I told her I'd have it and I fucking don't, and she needs it or she's leaving."

"Good God, man, get the fuck off my property."

"Please, Joey!"

"That's too fucking bad. Get off my property or I'll fucking kill you."

He finally left, and I later found out he tried bringing Vella to a bus stop to get him the fuck out of town. But on the way, he got pulled over for not having his headlights on. When the cops got up to his car to talk to him, they heard mumbling coming from the trunk, and it was fucking over. God bless his heart, Vella never ratted me out; it was fucking Steve, that cocksucker.

Meanwhile at home, I drank myself into a blackout; it was the only thing I could think to do. The next thing I remember is someone banging on the door frantically. It was morning.

A kid named Brady was on the other side of the door. He was a cool guy, an employee at the dealership who loved his weed.

"What's going on?" I asked him, opening the door.

"Joey, the cops got the dealership surrounded. They're on their way here."

"Are you fucking serious? Fuck."

"I wanted to give you a warning, but they're probably not far behind me," Brady said.

"Thanks a lot—here, take some weed as a thank you." I let him inside and pointed him in the direction of my stash. "I'm going to take a shower."

"Joey, they'll be here any minute. I'm serious."

"That's okay, that's okay . . . let me call Kathy." It's almost as if I wanted the cops to catch me, to just get this over with.

Kathy and I were on the outs again. We hadn't talked in a couple of days because she'd had a beauty school test I was supposed to be her hair model for and I never showed up. I figured I would try her anyway, in hopes she'd speak to me.

"Kathy, hey, something happened," I started explaining to her when she answered. "I need you to pick me up outside of King's in a half hour."

Realizing it was serious, she agreed, and I booked it over to King Soopers across the street, sending Brady on his own way, too. As I was waiting for Kathy, I realized I'd left my weed at home. Me being the savage I was, I *had* to go back and grab it. When I got back home, five cop cars were surrounding my place. I snuck around to the back of my house, out of their sight, and crawled through a window. I climbed back out, weed and pipe in hand, and got back to King's just as Kathy was pulling up.

Kathy's parents were out of the house for the weekend, so we headed there, to North Boulder. They wouldn't be back for a few days, which gave me time to get my head together. I called George from a pay phone the next day to fill him in.

"Dude, they're looking for you everywhere," he told me. "They were here, they went to the Chrysler store, they went to the Subaru store, they're searching grocery stores . . . you name it. One of the cops gave me his card and told me to call him if I found you."

"Give me the number," I said. "I'll call."

I knew my situation was bad, don't get me wrong, but I thought it was like any other thing I'd done in the past. I didn't really put that much stock in it. My New Jersey mentality had taken over. It was very much an "I didn't do anything wrong" way of thinking.

When I called the station, I explained who I was, and they immediately put me on hold to trace the pay phone. I hung up.

When I called back, they did it again.

"Don't put me on fucking hold," I said when I called back the third time. "I know what you guys are doing. I'm willing to turn myself in."

The line fell silent.

"Am I being charged with anything?" I asked.

"No, they just want to get your side of the story, just a few questions," the dispatcher said.

I thought about it for a second, not actually ready to give myself up.

"Instead of continuing to hang up and do this back and forth, why don't you just tell me where you are and someone will come pick you up?"

"Alright, I'm at Albertsons on Iris Ave," I lied.

"We'll be there soon."

Four minutes later, while I sat in my car across the street from Albertsons waiting to see how it would play out, I saw detective cars, a band of SWAT cars, and a giant police truck all swarming up.

Cops started running in and out of Albertsons trying to find me with no success.

"Holy shit," I said aloud to myself before pulling away. I went to a video store, rented two movies, stopped and got Chinese food, and then went back to Kathy's parents' house.

"Oh, God," she said when I walked in. "What happened?"

"I called the cops, just to see," I said. "They're really fucking looking for me out there."

"What are you going to do?"

"They're gonna catch me wherever the fuck I go," I said. "At least if I go down there on my own tomorrow, I can explain everything to them, help them understand my side. My innocence."

The next morning, I figured if I headed to the station, I'd get questioned and be home by 3 PM at the latest.

"Don Johnson is marrying Sheena Easton on *Miami Vice* tonight, and I want to see that wedding," I reminded Kathy, taking a bite of breakfast sausage. "Can you bring me to the station when we're done so I can get this over with?"

Kathy dropped me off and I asked her to grab me at the bus stop on the way back. I'd lost my fucking mind. I went upstairs to the Detective Bureau and rang the bell.

"Who is it?" someone shouted out.

"Jose Diaz."

They buzzed me in immediately, and by the time I walked in, six cops were standing there with their guns drawn.

"Get on the floor!" they all screamed. "Get on the floor!"

"Jose Diaz, you're being charged with one count of kidnapping, two counts of aggravated robbery, and second-degree burglary," one of the detectives said.

"No, no, kidnapping? I didn't kidnap nobody," I said from the ground. "You got the wrong guy."

I thought that kidnapping was when you tie someone up, throw them in a van, and hide them in a dungeon while sending their family ransom notes. Colorado law says that kidnapping is when you take a person from one location to another location—even just another room in the house—against their will. And that's just what we did.

The detective dragged me to my feet and handcuffed me. Everyone was yelling all at once. I wasn't sure who to listen to, so I stood there—hands behind my back—silently. One of the guys started emptying my pockets, quickly searching to make sure I didn't have a weapon on me.

"Do you want to make a statement?" the detective asked.

"Absolutely, I mean, I'm telling you . . . you've got the story completely wrong if you think it's me," I said.

They had me posted up in the detective room for what felt like for-fucking-ever before they walked in to hear my side.

"I was doing a drug deal, that was fucked up, yeah. But before I knew it, a gun was being pulled on me. I had no idea what was going on," I said. "I got the shakedown."

"So if you weren't involved, why didn't you call the cops afterward?" the detective asked smugly.

"I was scared," I lied. "I thought if I said anything, the guy would come back and shoot me."

"Yeah . . . that's not going to work for us," he said.

They didn't believe a word I was saying. They processed me, and I waited in that cell for six hours before I got an update.

"You'll be in front of a judge tomorrow," a cop told me through the bars. "He'll officially charge you then, and your bail will be set at fifty thousand. So unless you've got someone out there with fifty thousand cash—and it has to be *cash*—you can expect to be in jail for a while, Mr. Diaz."

My jaw dropped to the fucking ground. I was in deep.

"Fuck, you're not going to believe this shit," I said to Kathy when they let me make a call. "I'm going to miss Don Johnson's wedding tonight."

15

Jail

While sitting in my cell the first night after my arrest, I got to thinking about Zoraida. She and I hadn't been in touch for years—not since I'd only begun to scratch the surface of committing crimes. Cocaine had already absorbed my life back then, and I'd felt embarrassed and preoccupied. I started missing our regular check-ins, and before I knew it, it had been five months since we'd spoken. When I'd finally gotten the nerve to call her back, she asked me where the fuck I'd been: said the cops had raided her, she'd gotten a broken leg, and there was no one there for her.

I felt so terrible listening to her. I remember I was at a pay phone, and I just dropped the phone. I'd let my mom down, I'd let myself down, I'd let Zoraida down. It was a kick to the stomach knowing I'd disappeared on her after she'd been there for me through everything. I wanted to try harder, but when I called again a couple of weeks later, her phone was disconnected. I wasn't able to track her down, and we never spoke again.

Now posted up in jail, I wondered what Zoraida would think of me, if she was even alive still. I heard she'd gotten sick and was doing pretty shitty, but I'd never tried calling again. I wish I did.

Any part of me that still believed I was a good person was fading behind those bars.

The next day in front of the judge, I pleaded not guilty and was given a court-appointed attorney who was definitely not equipped to take on a case like mine. That cop had been right—my bail was set at fifty thousand dollars.

"How's Hercules?" I asked Kathy when she came to visit me. At least I'd been mostly good to that dog. "He doing okay?"

"He's fine," she said. "I just can't believe this, Joey. What are we going to do? I think we should tell my parents and see if my dad can help."

"Are you crazy?" I asked her. "He'll hate me for this."

I knew I needed someone of power in my corner, but I was petrified of that man. I mean, I'd taken his daughter on a whim to San Francisco with no warning; I'd missed his son's wedding because I'd been coked out of my mind; I'd disappointed Kathy again and again; and I'd landed here, in a fucking orange jumpsuit. Surely, he must hate me.

Kathy had two sisters, three brothers, and a ton of cousins, and I knew her dad, Ray, was the rock for every one of these people; everyone went to him. Kathy felt sure that, despite everything, he would be the rock for me, too. She went out to dinner with him to explain the situation.

"He wants to help," she told me over the phone after they'd discussed it. "He's going to come visit you and come up with a plan."

When he showed up, the whole conversation with him was fucking unbelievable, in a good way.

"Joey," he said, looking me dead in the eye, "you made a mistake. It happens. But this can all be fixed."

"I want you to listen to me every step of the way," he continued and started to tell me about one of his clients at the insurance company he worked for who'd gotten in trouble with the law because of drugs. "We got my client out, and we can get you out, too. That's the first step. Get you out of here on bail however we can, then cross the next bridge."

Ray pulled some strings and somehow managed to get my bail knocked down to three grand in a special hearing. I was out of jail after only two weeks. While we awaited my trial, Ray pushed me to get my high school diploma and to register for college—anything to help show the judge I was making strides to better my life.

I knew I needed to keep out of the cops' view. It was tough, considering they were also trying to wrongly pin the death of a local Spanish drug dealer on me. They were also trying to say I was involved in the case of a different drug dealer who'd gotten chased out of his apartment by someone trying to rob him, and when the drug dealer jumped out of the window, he broke both of his legs. Neither of them was my crime.

I had to go before the judge for my preliminary case at the end of January 1988, and I let him know I was actively looking for another attorney since my court-appointed attorney wasn't going to cut it. I once again pleaded not guilty. There was some paperwork they needed me to sign as I was leaving that day and—little did I know—I was about to get cornered.

I walked into the clerk's office, and two officers were sitting there with a stack of pictures, waiting for me. There in the stack were a ton of pictures of me in Snowmass Village selling drugs. I fucking *knew* I was being followed out there.

"Mr. Diaz, you were around some big-time dealers in Snowmass," the one cop said as he continued to toss pictures in front of me. "If you could help us by setting up a buy from them, we'll talk to the judge for you. We'll get him to lessen your time."

I sat there, waiting them out.

"All we'd need you to do is make a buy on a tape recorder," he continued. "It would help our investigation of these guys, and then you can move on with your life, too."

"Alright," I finally said. "I'll consider it."

I wasn't going to consider it, though. I wasn't a snitch—never was, never would be. I just wanted them to let me leave without any trouble that day. Soon after, though, I got a call from someone from the DEA.

"I'm your point guy," he told me. "Let's make this happen."

"That's not going to fucking happen, man," I told him. "I have a job, I'm taking classes, I'm doing good. I'm going to be fine with the judge.

"I appreciate what you're saying to me," I continued, "but I'm going to beat this case."

They never bothered me about it again. To stay on track, I got a job at Hertz detailing cars, and they ended up putting me into a manager's training program. I also joined the Boulder Masters Swimming program. I was going there three days a week at 6 AM to swim for an hour, trying to revamp myself all around.

But I had to at least *try* to fuck it up.

I started shoplifting at the mall near me. At the time, Bruce Springsteen had a box set out and it was always on display in Sears. So I would walk in and grab two or three and then sell them to a local record store for sixty bucks, brand new. I kept this going for about a month that summer, every day. It was as simple as if I was getting it from an ATM. I'd just go in to take money out. And then I started getting greedy. One day I went in and took about ten of the box sets. Then I heard a security guard.

"Hey!" he screamed. "What the fuck are you doing?"

I started running while he was chasing me on a scooter. As I was running, I was tossing the records at him hoping to slow him down or, better yet, knock him down. He must have signaled for the cops somehow because, by the time I got outside, there was a cop car waiting for me.

"Un-fucking-believable," I said, throwing my hands in the air.

I knew I couldn't give up who I was. There's no way this could be good for a guy out on bail. They took me down to the police station, but I'd known not to bring my license with me for these shoplifting excursions, so when they asked my name, I gave them a fake one: James Smith. By the time they were ready to release me on my own recognizance that night, they told me I needed to have someone come pick me up, and they needed to bring my license.

"You're not going to believe this," I told them. "I actually lost my license. I don't have one right now."

"Well, if you don't have a license to show us, you at least need someone to come in here and identify you," the cop said. "There's the phone— give them a call."

I grabbed the phone and dialed Kathy.

"Hello?" she answered.

"Hi, this is James Smith," I said. "We went out last week . . ."

"Joey? Is that you?"

"It's *James Smith*. Is there any chance you can come down to Boulder police station and identify me?"

"I'll be there in fifteen minutes." She didn't ask another question.

Because I had a knack for making friends with people wherever I went, I'd become friendly with one of the guards at the station when I'd been locked up there, and of course he was standing around while I was getting fingerprinted.

"What's up, Joey? How've you been?" he asked, ignoring that I was clearly brought in there for a fresh crime.

"I'm great, man, yeah, I'm great . . ."

He reached in to give me a hug, and I prayed he wouldn't see the card with the wrong name. Let him think I was getting charged again as me, not James Smith.

"Yes, I can identify him," Kathy told the police officer when she got there, the guard now gone from the scene. "This is James Smith."

"Alright," he said to us. "That'll do it then. You're free to go for now, but hey, make sure you get a new license, okay? You need a form of ID, James."

"Got it, absolutely."

By the time my court date came around for James's crime, I stuck with the lost license story and went in front of the judge (luckily a different judge) as James. He fined me a hundred bucks and twenty hours of community service, which I did in full as James at an HIV/AIDS center. No one ever connected that it was me.

As my kidnapping trial approached, Ray and I got people to write hundreds of letters to the judge to justify that I was a good, decent member of the community. Surprisingly, people wrote them without hesitation. No one wanted me to go to jail, especially Ray. I also got my GED, like Ray suggested, and enrolled in a program for minorities at the University of Colorado.

My trial took place in August of 1988, and I felt confident heading in. The morning of, I put on my Armani suit I had dry-cleaned special for this occasion, and I went down to the courthouse. If there were fifty people in that courtroom, forty-three of them were there to support me. When my name was called, I shot Kathy and her family a look.

"We got this," I mouthed to them.

"Alright, Mr. Diaz, let's see here," the judge said, skimming through a stack of papers. "I see you have a lot of support here for you today . . ."

"Yes, sir," I said. The judge handling my case was strict, and when I found out he had a brother who lived locally and was a dentist, I scoured the area for anyone who was a patient. A friend of mine had been going to him, so I had my friend make an appointment, go in, and put in a good word for me.

I was pulling out *every* stop.

My attorney and I knew ahead of time that the maximum sentencing I could get was six years, but I could *possibly* get nothing. I had no idea what to expect.

"Alright, do you have anything to say?"

I froze. Like, completely froze. I can talk to any person at any time about anything . . . and here I was, speechless.

"Okay, I'll take that as a no," he said after a long pause. "Mr. Diaz, I'm sentencing you to four years in the Department of Corrections."

"Oh, my God," I finally said aloud. I quickly turned to Kathy. The look on her face matched what I'm sure the look on my face was, too—fucking horror.

"Your honor," my attorney said. "As you may know, Mr. Diaz is enrolled in the University of Colorado and we would like to give him a few days to get in touch with the school and let them know what's going on before you process him."

"No," the judge said without skipping a beat. "Four years, Department of Corrections, case closed. He'll be booked today."

They handcuffed me immediately, right in front of my friends and family. It was one of the worst moments of my life, without a doubt. As I was walking away, the judge motioned for me to come over.

"Mr. Diaz, don't forget to submit a reconsideration in three months, on December 15," he said. I nodded, semi-relieved by the thought that I could get out sooner than in four years. But the feeling of not knowing—and potentially being stuck in jail for four fucking years—was brutal.

I gave Kathy a half-hug, the best I could do with handcuffs on, and nodded to the rest of my people as the guards pulled me away.

As I was being walked through the hallway, I saw the sight of all sights. Reggie—that fucking cocksucker—was standing there in a trustee uniform mopping the floor. Trustees were inmates who were considered high on the food chain, so to speak, so the fact that Reggie was a trustee let me in on one major fact that I guess I'd already known: Reggie was the one who'd ratted me out. Now, he was getting special treatment for it.

"Yep," the one guard read my mind. "That guy's a rat."

They walked me to a cell and closed the door. I sat down on the bench in my eight-hundred-dollar suit, in disbelief. I went to take off my jacket and felt something in my pocket. It was a fucking rock of coke. I crushed it up and snorted the whole thing in one go. I don't remember passing out, just that when a guard came back in hours later to get me, I was lying down with my shoes off and my jacket on top of me like a blanket.

"Wake up, you piece of shit." The guard shoved me. "You're going to county jail."

I talked to Ray on the phone the first chance I got, and he was set on getting me out.

"I'm going to try the governor's office and a few other contacts who might get us to the top of the food chain here," he told me. "I'm also going to . . ."

"Ray, I appreciate your help more than I can say, but I'm here now," I told him. "I've accepted my punishment."

"We're going to keep putting in as much work as we can on our end," he assured me. "We'll figure something out. For now, be safe in there."

With systems backed up, I was told I would stay in county jail until December or January, depending on when space cleared up. All hope was gone, as far as I saw it, and I had to accept my time like a man. I'd done bad shit for a long, long time—for many of my twenty-five years on earth. This was coming to me. I had to put my big boy pants on.

———

The first day of county jail was actually great. I made a few friends, and they filled me in on what to expect. They were nice people. But, I only ended up being there a few days before they told me to pack my shit; I was moving to a different county jail at a ski resort. That next jail was a fucking country club. It was in the mountains of Colorado, and it was beautiful. As soon as I got there, I met a guy from New York who taught me how to play handball. I fit right in with the rest of the guys, too. We just hung out all day outside—we were allowed to be out there all fucking day. At dinnertime, we came inside to eat, and then we were allowed to go back out in the yard until shower time at 8 PM. Then it was TV time at 9 PM, and then at 10 PM the guards would take a money collection and go to Safeway for us and bring back whatever we wanted. Yoo-hoos, chocolate, popcorn, pizza.

This was nothing like I pictured jail to be. There were only like twelve of us total locked up in the entire place. It was a fucking party, and I was happy when they told me I'd be there for four months. But, I was barely there a couple of weeks before they shipped me off again.

Now, I went to the Department of Corrections, where I had to spend a week in diagnostic. In diagnostic, they test everything. They do every physical and mental evaluation possible. I'm fucking terrified of needles, so when the needle came out for blood work, I figured I was fucked.

"I'm scared of needles," I told the nurse. "I'll probably faint."

"You'll be fine . . ." she said, glancing at my paperwork, "Okay, Mr. Diaz, here we go."

I sat there in what looked like a classroom, filled with school desks, and asked the nurse if I could lie down while she drew my blood. In fact, I needed her to open the window, too, to give me some air. She drew the blood and . . . nothing. I folded my arm back up and made it back to my cell in the South Tower.

"I can't believe it," I said to one of the guys I'd become friendly with that week. "I'm actually fine. I didn't pass out."

I unfolded my arm, took off the cotton ball they'd jammed in between the fold of my arm, and there it was . . . a drop of blood. I hit the ground. I woke up in the prison hospital with a bag of ice on my head—but, thankfully my shit was still intact, if you know what I mean. I knew if no one had taken advantage of me then, while I'd been passed out, I'd be safe.

That week gave them a very thorough evaluation of me. The feds now knew everything about me—they had *everything*. And, being at the Department of Corrections was tough. This was what I thought jail would be . . . fistfights were happening, people were yelling all night across the entire place—sometimes taking the water out of their toilets so they could talk through them to each other on different floors. Not to mention inmates were fucking stabbing each other. It was brutal.

When I was done there, they found a permanent home for me at Camp George West in Golden, Colorado. It was only about thirty minutes from Kathy, which was good. Camp George West was just as it sounds, a former army base. At one point it had been converted into a prison, but it was still set up like army barracks. There were no cells.

My first stop when I got there was to see my counselor, a dude named Mr. Blue.

"Hey, I'm . . ." I started to say when I walked into his office.

"Shut up," he immediately said and directed me to sit down. "Diaz, huh? What kind of name is that?"

"It's Cuban."

"Spanish, okay. Understand when I tell you this, I don't like spics, so I don't like you too much."

I sat there quietly, but I guess I grinned.

"You can take that fucking smile off your face, Mr. Diaz. Have you ever had hepatitis?"

"No."

"Perfect. Your job's gonna be in the kitchen. Get the fuck out of my office."

I got up and walked out, not really knowing what just happened.

I didn't last long at my first gig there. I was introduced to Mr. Yarborough, a former Navy dude, who would be my boss. He was a big dude—like six-six, three hundred pounds, and no sense of humor.

"I expect to see you in the mornings at 6 AM sharp," he told me. "You're my new baker. I figured Italian people can bake."

"Okay, uhhh, I'm not Italian, though," I told him. "I'm Cuban."

"Well, that's too bad. I'll see you at six."

My first assignment was to make cinnamon buns. I didn't know what the fuck I was doing. I tried to follow Mr. Yarborough's instructions. I put the buns in the oven just like he showed me, and I sat and waited. The next thing I know I smelt fire, and I ran to the oven. I guess I made the buns too big because they'd blown up to the size of manhole covers. The whole fucking thing was in flames.

Mr. Yarborough came in screaming. "What the fuck! You're fired! Get out of my sight."

I was reassigned to stock clerk for the kitchen, which turned out to be the best job in the entire place, no kidding. My job was to figure out what the kitchen needed in the mornings, grab whatever it was from storage, and bring the food back to the kitchen. I was also responsible for ordering food for the kitchen. I had no boss, and it set me up real nice to have access to everything coming into the jail's kitchen—hamburgers, chicken, fries—and I could steal anything I wanted. I became an instant friend to everyone who had something to hide, especially drugs like steroids, because my storage area was the perfect place. I was put into a position of power.

Believe it or not, I was happy in jail. It also felt good to be off the coke. My head wasn't constantly fucking throbbing.

My job only took an hour or so, so by early morning I was already done for the day. I'd go in around 8 AM, leave around 9 AM, then I'd go to the library to read the paper. There were two other inmates who were always around the library with me. The guy who worked at the library, the librarian, was this geeky guy: a bookworm who was there for killing his wife and the mailman when he caught them having an affair. He was very smart but had a dangerous, wicked smile. I'll never forget the time he said to me, "Think of all the time you wasted with drugs. What would happen if you put that same energy you put into drugs into bettering your life?"

The other dude was in charge of the kitchen, and they called him Chicken Hawk. Chicken Hawk was covered in freckles and had a gold tooth. He would dress in all white—as the kitchen staff was supposed to—a stark contrast to his dark skin color. His Jheri curl was always fucked up, sticking directly up in the air. He'd committed murder, too, but I only found out weeks after first meeting him, since he was a man of few words.

As a Cuban guy in jail, it could have been very isolating if I let it be. But I didn't. There were usually rifts between the Blacks, the Mexicans, the bikers, the heroin junkies. My gift was that I could run with any of these crews; they all liked me.

In fact, the whole time I was at Camp George West, there was only one dude who got under my skin. He was part of the biker gang and he thought he was the shit, but really he was a moron. He worked in the kitchen, and whenever I'd walk by, he'd have to make a fucking scene with stupid comments directed at me. I got tired of him, so I took a wholesale-sized American cheese box that was lying around—one of those long, thin boxes—and I took a huge shit in it. I closed it up and put it in a drawer in his bunk under a bunch of his clothes.

"It smells like shit in my room, doesn't it?" he kept asking everyone who bunked around us. "Where the fuck is that smell coming from?"

The day he finally found it, this guy was fucking furious. Later down the road, when I realized that hadn't fully gotten him off my back, I had to beat him to a pulp. He never fucking bothered me again after that one.

Everyone else I crossed paths with seemed to like me because I had something to offer them. I found out, too, that when you're funny—you just say shit like it is—people like you in there. Every Wednesday the inmates were allowed to get together to watch a movie, but the projector was constantly broken.

"Get up and tell us a joke, Cuba," the librarian shouted one Wednesday night as someone poked around with the projector. "What else do we got to do?"

I figured, what the fuck, so I stood up in front of the guys and just went off. I said any and everything that came to my mind. Racial slurs, an endless string of cursing, roasting every person in the room who I didn't think would stab me to death after I was done. *Cocksucker this. Cocksucker that.* And the room was in an uproar—we were all laughing our asses off.

From then on, they'd beg me to do "stand-up" on Wednesdays. I didn't have written jokes; it was mostly just me continuing to talk shit, and my little crowd there loved it. People told me I was funny my whole life—I'm a no-filter kind of guy—but I never thought much of it. Now, I was rocking and rolling with comedy in a way, and part of me wondered how fun this would be as a career. It seemed like a total long shot.

I thought: "Imagine just getting up onstage, saying a bunch of funny shit, making people laugh, and *that* is your *job*. It would almost be too good to be true." Before I knew it, I was living for those Wednesday nights, to get up there and just let loose. Who figured I would have found the career path I was destined for behind fucking bars?

On the more serious side, though, jail also gave me plenty of time to wrap my head around why I deserved to be there. It let me take some time for self-awareness that I'd never really given myself before. Every inmate had a report from that week in diagnostic that, in part, broke down some findings about their character. All the other inmates had theirs, but I never saw mine, so in the weekly meetings I had to have with Mr. Blue, I kept asking him what was up.

"Where is that report from diagnostic?" I'd press him. "I really want to see what it says."

"You can't handle what that report says," he finally told me after weeks of me hounding him.

"What the fuck do you mean?" I asked. "I can't handle it? What are you talking about?"

He said nothing.

"What's up with that report? You need to tell me."

"You're not going to let up on this are you?" he said.

"Never."

Mr. Blue walked over to his desk, pulled out the file, and stared at it.

"Alright, here's the abbreviated version," he said. "What it says on here is that if I have something you want, I might as well just give it to you because you're going to take it from me anyway."

I stood there, letting his words soak in. I was upset. After examining me at the core from all aspects, they found that scientifically I was—and would always be—*a thief*.

"Thank you for your time," I finally said, walking out.

A few days later, after avoiding Craine, he came up to me as I was loading a truck with lunches for the inmates who were assigned to pick up trash along the roads.

"I haven't seen you around much," Craine said. "I told you that you couldn't handle what was in that report."

"No, I just couldn't handle you calling me a thief," I said, refusing to face him.

"I didn't call you a thief," he assured me. "You're reading too fucking deep into my words. What I said was that you're a dangerous person. And that's because if you want something, you can get it. That's what I told you, you fuck. But you're too stupid of a fucking spic to understand these things."

I kept loading the truck, trying my best to understand.

"What I'm telling you is when you get out of here, you got the world at your feet," Craine continued. "If you want it, it's yours. You just have to apply yourself. You can get whatever you want. You're *that smart*."

I was blown the fuck away by what he was saying.

"When you get out of here, go find something you want to give a hundred percent to and do it. It's going to pay off for you."

There I was thinking this guy hated me, thought I was the dumbest immigrant he'd ever met, and really he was thinking just the opposite.

"Now for the bigger news," he said. I was already stopped in my tracks paying close attention to him. "Your paperwork has been cleared with a halfway house. You're all set to go."

While I'd been locked up, House Bill 1200 was passed, and it benefitted prisoners who'd committed a first offense, non-violent crime, myself included. This meant my time was cut from forty-eight to twenty-four months right off the bat. Unexpectedly now, per Craine, I was eligible for a halfway house around my six-month mark.

A few days before my twenty-sixth birthday that February, I said my goodbyes. My last day at Camp George West, I thought about Mr. Blue's words, about what the librarian said to me too about bettering my life, and about my time locked up as a whole. I considered if there was anything I could give a hundred percent of myself to—something to get me away from drugs long-term, away from a life of pure crime, and onto a better, happier path.

When I was leaving, the librarian handed me a blank notebook.

"I want you to use this and start writing your jokes down," he said. "When I get out of here in a few years, you better be a comedian. Because if you're not, I'm gonna kill you."

"Hmm," I thought to myself. "I don't think he's fucking kidding."

16

A Catholic in Conflict

On the flight to our honeymoon in San Francisco, right after we'd had sex on the plane, I realized I wasn't in love with Kathy anymore. Not real love anyway; maybe a type of love you have for someone you've known a while but definitely not the kind of love people should get married over.

We'd been together for what felt like forever, and Kathy had stuck with me through everything. So when she accidentally got pregnant after we fucked in the bushes in her parents' yard about three months after I got out of jail, I figured the right thing to do was to propose. I heard my mom's voice echoing in my head: "I just want you to be a man." I was hoping this would count: me growing up, getting a wife, and raising a child. I could do this, I told myself. I could surely be *happy* doing this. It was the American way.

I realized too late that when you marry someone, you should have that *feeling*. That one that you'd do anything for that person. You'd jump off a bridge for them. But I didn't have that with Kathy. Things weren't romantic at all anymore after I got out of jail. We were just going through the motions—we weren't head over heels for each other. The only thing I was head over heels for was cocaine.

My behavior had been almost perfect in jail—a few hits of acid here and there, maybe a little meth, like three times. All in all, I was fucking good. Being in there for a few months added years to my life. But, after jail, my bad habits were once again on the upswing. (Strangely enough, the halfway house they sent me to was the one across the street from where I'd hidden the coke on the day of the kidnapping. That, and the fact that my attorney fees ended up being eighteen thousand bucks—the exact amount I'd made from selling that coke—made it seem like the universe was trying to tell me something: I *needed* to get busted.)

At the halfway house, I was back on my cocaine game. I came out of the gate fucking swinging. I was the old Joey Diaz. The first day in the halfway house they made you stay inside for twenty-four hours straight. They evaluated you and asked you a bunch of creepy questions and showed you your room. After that, you were allowed to leave only for therapy and work—whatever job you could find—but you had to give them a number where they could find you at any time. They didn't let you get too comfortable. To get around the strict rules, I told them I was working as an independent car detailer—so if they ever couldn't get ahold of me—it was *only* because I was in a car cleaning it up.

I wasn't allowed to have my own car, but I got one anyway. We weren't allowed to have drugs in the halfway house, of course, but I brought in coke and a scale anyway. I wasn't too scared to break their rules. I thought I could talk my way out of anything, God forbid. I'd say about fifty percent of the people in that place had a substance abuse problem, so I figured that there were plenty of other people for them to worry about.

Despite what I was up to, I was able to stay on their good side, and within a month, my "good" behavior moved me to a higher level, as they referred to it. Every level you moved up gave you more freedoms, like being able to stay out later at night and go out on the weekends. My goal was to work up the levels, stay out of trouble, and get the fuck out of there.

I was still in the halfway house when Kathy found out she was pregnant—but all seemed fine, especially because I had this idea in my head that being a dad would be a walk in the park. I didn't consider what being a dad would mean for my lifestyle.

When Kathy and I got married on September 9, 1989, at Sacred Heart Church in Boulder, I'd just gotten out of the halfway house. I was still on probation, but the judge was nice enough to let me leave the state for our honeymoon in San Francisco. Getting hit with the harsh reality that I was now stuck as a husband—and that I wasn't actually in love with my wife—my cocaine habit skyrocketed again. A month after our honeymoon, I failed a drug test and I was sent back to the halfway house. Maybe subconsciously I didn't want to live in a two-bedroom apartment together with my wife, while we waited for a kid. Maybe I secretly *wanted* to get caught to get away from her.

They put me in an outpatient rehab program, too, and I had to start going from 6 to 9 PM five nights a week, on top of working full time. My time in the halfway house—originally only supposed to be another ninety days—kept getting extended because I was a fuckup. I didn't end up getting out until February, and Kathy was about to pop.

The day I was released, Kathy came and picked me up, and we went to a Cajun restaurant to celebrate. The baby was due in two weeks, which I thought gave us some time to get settled together again, whether I wanted to or not.

We ate, dozed off, and around 5:30 in the morning, Kathy woke me up.

"My water broke!" She was clenching her stomach and looking around frantically.

"Huh?" I asked. "What's that?"

"I'm going to have the baby!" she screamed.

We both started getting our shit together while I glanced outside. A fucking foot of snow had piled up overnight. I went to shovel the car out and dig a path for Kathy. It took like twenty minutes, and as soon as I cleared a space for her to get in, my neighbor who was a total mother-fucker, pulled into it.

"What the fuck, dude?" I said. "I need to get my wife in here. She's in labor."

He got out of his car, didn't say a word, then walked over and spit on my bumper.

Next thing you know, I was fist fighting this guy. We were wrestling in the snow as Kathy shouted for us to stop; she needed to get to a doctor quick. We were only fighting a few minutes before a couple of cop cars rolled up. One of them came running up and grabbed me off this prick.

"What's happening here?" the cop said. "We got a call reporting domestic violence. Said they heard a woman screaming."

"No, no, not domestic violence; my wife's in labor," I corrected him. "And this fuck . . ." I pointed at my neighbor, lying bloody in the snow, before explaining what happened. The cops looked around taking in the situation as I wondered whether this brawl would land me in jail while Kathy was delivering this baby.

"Alright," one of the cops finally said. "Let's just chalk this up to a bad morning for both of you. Shake hands, and let's end this."

I shook the dickhead's hand and got Kathy in the car, finally. The cops were nice enough to help us out. One cop car went ahead of me, and the other behind, and they got us to the hospital in no time.

Kathy was a granola chick; she always wanted to have the baby naturally with a birthing coach at this specialty place in Boulder. Now, under the gun, she canned that idea real quick. The hospital was the only choice. I suited up in the hospital gown and that little fucking hat they give you and headed into the delivery room with her, praying to God I wouldn't see any blood and pass out. Luckily, both of us did great, and on February 3, 1990, we brought our nine-pound little girl, Jackie, into the world. On the outside, I seemed great; I was handling all of this in stride. On the inside, I was freaking the fuck out. Holding her in my arms, I instantly knew I couldn't cover the spread here. How the fuck was *I* going to be a good father?

I didn't quit coke because of the baby; I needed the drugs. I just started finding more creative ways around the testing system so I could stay out of trouble. Word on the street was that if you drank a mixture of cranberry juice, the powder you use to make Jell-O, and apple cider vinegar, it would tamper with your drug test results, and lo and behold it fucking worked.

Over time, my methods for messing with the tests became a little less conventional. Like, I went to the pool store and bought chlorine pills, the ones you drop in the pool to clean it. What I'd do is grind them up into a powder, and when I was on my way to take a piss test, I'd pull back the skin on my uncircumcised dick and sprinkle the powder in there. I'd put a rubber band to secure it in. At the test, I'd throw the rubber band off in my pants and pull the skin back and pee. The chlorine powder would fall into the piss and I'd be set—the test sample would be fucked. The people at the testing center couldn't figure it out.

"This has to stop, Mr. Diaz," the head of the drug testing facility told me. "You're doing something to mess with this test."

"I swear I'm not!" I assured her. "They watch me pee. What could I possibly be doing?"

The time I tried the same trick with Drano, it made the pee sample start smoking up in the bottle. No one besides me noticed, and I was cracking the fuck up as it bubbled. That sample ended up breaking their machine.

To answer the question you probably have . . . yes, my dick got so scarred up from this shit.

And to answer your other question, *yes*, this is what the father of a newborn baby was up to.

———

Other than the drugs—or maybe partly because of them—I was completely and totally unhappy. I took a job with Kathy's family's roofing company, and it was the only thing bringing me any happiness. Deep down, I knew the marriage was the main problem, but I wouldn't let myself come to terms with it. I didn't have the balls to get divorced—Catholics didn't do that. I made it my mission to be happy in other parts of my life to try to outweigh my troubles at home, and to not be a bad Catholic.

In fact, I *turned to* religion. A man in my late twenties, I went and got my confirmation at the Catholic church because I thought maybe Jesus would guide me out of this funk—whatever it was that was bothering me in my core. When that didn't work, I tried Buddhism. I even wore a fucking robe and everything. I also tried rehab and therapy. Some court-appointed, others on my own. I meditated every day. I'd close my eyes and give myself a blank slate in my mind. I'd try to block out the thoughts of my unhappy marriage, or feeling *stuck*. I'd use the time to focus on the good things—my daughter, for one.

None of it worked. I hated being home unless it was to spend time with Jackie. Eventually I think Kathy started picking up on it.

"Maybe you need a vacation," she said to me over dinner one night. "Why don't you go home and visit your friends for a few days?"

I hadn't been to Jersey in six years. I'd sworn it off, figuring it was the root of my life's problems (hah!) and it would be better to avoid the place altogether. Now, anything was worth a try.

The whole week I was there, I mostly drank and did drugs with my buddies, but I also got to spend some time with Juan. Being a dad—or at least trying to—had given me a push to reconnect with him. It had been years since we'd spoken, but when I saw him on this trip back to Jersey, it was like no time at all had passed. He invited me over for dinner, and I could tell he was genuinely happy to see me. I was genuinely happy to see him, too (though I brought a gun with me just in case).

"I look back, and I realize how hard it must have been for you," he admitted. "You lost a lot very early in life."

"It sucked, yeah," I said. "I know losing her was hard for you, too."

There was a ton more to say, but we didn't really need to say it for it to be heard. It was clear to me now that he and I were both on the same page—and it was a good one. When I was leaving, he gave me some jewelry for the baby. It felt like a peace offering, and I was glad to make the peace.

It was a great trip to say the least, but back in Colorado, I went back to feeling like shit almost immediately. But then it happened: a miracle from God. After a little over two years of soul-sucking marriage and many failed attempts at finding any sort of personal happiness, Kathy called me into the kitchen. She was holding out a piece of paper.

"What's this?" she asked, pissed off, clearly.

"Umm, let me see," I said, taking it from her and reading it over. "This is from a school loan I took out last year. I needed the money to buy a car. But, it's paid off."

"I'm your wife. You should have told me if you were taking out a loan, regardless of what it was for," she said, followed by words that were music to my ears. "This isn't working for me, Joey. I think it's time we separate for a while."

And there it was. Kathy—the person who I'd come to feel nothing for—gave me the greatest gift of all: she set me free.

PART 3

Comedy

17

Do You Want to Be a Stand-up Comic?

As much as my marriage to Kathy had me in fucking misery, I'll hand it to her on one account: if it wasn't for her, I would have never gotten on a real stage to do comedy. I mentioned all the hell I was going through with her, but in the middle of all that, she gave me a push I needed.

Comedy was front of mind for me when I was leaving jail, but life happened, and I'd gotten distracted. Then, one day when Kathy and I were still together, I was home watching the Tom Hanks movie, *Punchline*—a movie about stand-up comedy.

"I really want to do comedy," I told Kathy afterwards. "I've been looking in the yellow pages for clubs that might let me do an open mic night or something. Looks like Comedy Works in Denver does open mic nights on Tuesdays."

She was very supportive of the idea from that second on.

"I think you should go for it," she said. "You would make a great comedian."

Comedy Works's process worked like this: You'd call them on a Monday, and they'd put you on the lineup for the following Tuesday if they had room. In general, open mics were open to people of any skill level in comedy; you didn't need any sort of name, they let anyone have a go. I got in the habit of getting my name on the list, and then cancelling on the day of. I was scared shitless to get up onstage.

Around this time, I was at work one morning, and my brother-in-law asked me to go grab breakfast for the guys. I went down the street to get some sandwiches and, while I was waiting for the order, I picked up a copy of *Rocky Mountain News* that was sitting there. I flipped it open to a random page, and smack in the middle of the page was a picture of Roseanne Barr next to an article headlined: "Do you want to be a stand-up comic?"

I couldn't fucking believe it. The article was about Roseanne's comedy career and the comedy scene in Denver. It talked about what you needed to do if you wanted to really do comedy: start at an open mic night. The article also recommended a comedy class on Sundays that was only thirty-three bucks at the University of Colorado. I decided to sign up on the spot.

On the last night of the course, after a few weeks of classes and practice, we had to perform in front of everyone. At the end of the class, the teacher pulled me aside.

"Hey, I'm going to be honest here," he said. "You're the only one in this class who has a real chance at this."

It was like a Mr. Blue moment for me.

"Wow, thanks so much," I said.

"Do you need help getting onstage?" he asked.

"Yeah, I don't really know where to start."

"Do me a favor. They're opening a club in Westminster. Go down there tomorrow—I'll call the owner in advance—and ask for a job as a door guy. It'll be good to get your foot in the door and go from there."

So that's what I did. I kept my roofing job and started working nights down at that club manning the door—and eventually taking over for a sound guy and a barback who'd both quit. One day, I finally got the nerve to ask the club owner if I could do a guest spot, and this fucking guy looked at me like I had three heads.

"Absolutely not," he told me.

I was so upset, but it gave me a push. Fuck this guy. If he wasn't going to give me stage time, I'd get it somewhere else. The next day I called Comedy Works to get added to the open mic night the following Tuesday. Kathy must have overheard my conversation, because a few days later she came up to me excited.

"Guess what?" she asked with a huge smile. "I got my mother to babysit on Tuesday. I'm going to drive you to Comedy Works and watch you perform."

This was the bind I needed. I got some jokes together—basically, I started writing in a notebook, jotting down a bunch of ideas and thoughts that came to mind, including some stuff I'd practiced in my comedy class. Then, I refined the jokes from there. In jail, my shtick was pretty much to just talk shit, and that worked on that crowd. But I knew getting up on a real stage, at a real comedy club, meant I needed a plan. I'd watched enough comedy in my life to be able to sort of mimic the cadence of a few of my favorites—mixing some Rodney Dangerfield,

Richard Pryor, and a little Andrew Dice Clay—and use my own jokes to execute the set. I had no idea what the fuck I was doing, but I figured I'd give it my best shot.

When Kathy and I got to Comedy Works, I looked around the room to see what I was up against. There were like twenty or thirty people there maybe, which . . . *fuck* . . . that wasn't a ton, but I'd never been so nervous in my entire life. I was pacing, sweating, cursing; I knew I needed to get past this first set if I wanted any chance at this. Lots of people talk about wanting to be a comic, but then they let this very moment stop them because they're scared. I couldn't let that be me.

When they called my name, I got up onstage, took a deep breath, and . . . *"What's up, you bad motherfuckers!"*

I couldn't tell you what I said, exactly. It doesn't really matter, because all I remember is hearing laughs coming from everywhere in the room. These people were laughing at *my* jokes. Getting offstage, I was even more sure that this was what I wanted to do with my life. All that nervousness had turned to pure fucking joy.

After my set, the club owner—a guy named Ed Nichols—and a bunch of other comics came up to me.

"That was great," Ed said. "Your stage presence is fucking brilliant. Was that really your first time doing stand-up?"

"It was, yeah," I said, in disbelief of how well it had gone. My head was buzzing. I was filled with adrenaline, I could barely think. But I'll tell you the truth—it was better than any drug, any rush I'd had in my crazy-ass life. I knew right away that when I was onstage, I was home.

"You're going to come back, right?" he asked.

"Fuck yeah, I'll be back."

A guy named Bill Bauer, who'd seen my set that night, called and asked me if I wanted to do five minutes at a comedy show at the Denver Broncos training facility. High on the experience, I said yes. I did some of the same material I'd used at Comedy Works. It killed again, whatever it was. After the show I got to spend time with the other comics, and it was like hanging out with fucking Jesus's disciples. Now I really had the bug.

In the middle of all of this was when Kathy left. The day I helped her pack her car, I was thanking God she simplified this whole thing. I should have been sad; I knew that. I should have looked at myself and been like, "What the fuck did I do to make this woman leave?" But I didn't. I didn't care.

I wasn't fully shocked, either. She also wasn't happy. Everything had been slowly catching up to her: my drug use, the lies, the fucking kidnapping. I imagine that the day she finally left me, Kathy was sure I'd never amount to anything. We agreed to stay civil, not date anyone, and decide in about a month whether we'd officially get divorced.

Meanwhile, my life was getting better by the second. I fully committed to comedy and was on the lookout for any opportunity for a gig. I was skimming the newspaper one day and saw something about a local amateur comedy contest. I called the guy running it, and he told me to come down for the first round.

I went . . . and I won. Two weeks later I showed up for round two and won again. Boulder wasn't a big comedy town, so I'd been having trouble finding places to regularly practice. That said, I couldn't believe I made it past two rounds of this contest. Really, I'd mostly been snagging the mic at poetry nights or karaoke bars, just to get onstage (and almost immediately thrown out). To perfect my skill, I'd rent videos of comics to study the art. I rented these Rodney Dangerfield and *Def Comedy Jam* tapes so many times that the video store stopped charging me. Now, as I waited for the final round of the contest, I was motivated as fuck, so I was constantly jotting down jokes and ideas, coming up with new material all day, every day.

Focusing on comedy felt easy until my separation with Kathy took a turn for the worse. She showed up one day and took literally *everything* out of our apartment—from furniture to silverware, to art on the wall.

"I'm confused here," I said to her on the phone that night. "You left me nothing. I'm looking at a milk crate that I have left to sit on. Let's see, a mattress without a box spring, no fucking towels and, what's this?" I asked opening the refrigerator. "Nothing in the fridge, either. You even took the mustard. Who takes the fucking mustard?"

"It's nothing personal," she said. "I need to get my own place, so I need all of those things."

"So this means there's no chance of us getting back together—trying that month break idea?" I asked.

"No, I think we need to move forward with a divorce," she said.

That was fine by me. I just didn't want to play these fucking games when it came to my stuff. She even took a Cuban memento that a friend gave me and sold it at a fucking yard sale. She was roasting me.

I kept my focus on the comedy contest. People were saying I was a top contender, plus I had an extra little trick up my sleeve to win. I was selling Valium at the time, and that meant I knew a lot of fucking people. I knew winners in this contest were determined by how much the audience applauded them, so the night of the finals I told all my Valium customers to come to the show for their next buy . . . and to make some fucking noise.

It was my turn to have Jackie the day of the final contest round, and Kathy knew how important that night would be for me. She was supposed to pick up the kid by seven so I could get down to the show by 8 PM. Kathy didn't show up until twenty minutes to eight, on fucking principle.

"You know I have my contest tonight," I said, handing Jackie over. "Where have you been?"

"Sorry, I was on a date," she said.

I carried the kid to her car, got in mine, and sped out of there fuming.

When I finally got to the contest, some punk who was competing against me that night almost got me disqualified, saying I wasn't an amateur comic. He called out that I was paid five bucks for gas money for the Broncos training facility show—asshole just didn't want to lose to me. Despite his bitching, the guy running the contest didn't count that gas money as a real comedy paycheck; he knew I was an amateur. They let me onstage without a problem. But getting up there, I was a little pissed off from that cocksucker trying to get me disqualified, and about Kathy. Adrenaline was pumping through my veins. If I'd been nervous at all, it was the last emotion I was feeling now. In comedy I've found that being a little pissed while up onstage can work in your favor—it gives you the right edge—and this was the first time I witnessed that in play.

Again, I can't remember exactly what I said onstage, but it must have been good enough. The applause I got after my set was fucking tremendous. When they announced me as the official winner and handed me a check for five hundred bucks, I knew my dream was really in the works now.

Instead of going home and celebrating with a ton of booze and drugs as I otherwise would have, I went home and let my mind soberly absorb it all. I had to put *everything* I had into this. That night I pulled out a few books I had on comedy and, from then on—in addition to all my other efforts—I started reading everything I could on stand-up.

Comedy was going to be the thing to keep me alive, even in times I'd be holding on by a thread.

18

What Does 'Spic' Mean?

I wanted to be a great dad for Jackie, but I sucked at it. In true Joey Diaz fashion, I couldn't get out of my own way. I loved Jackie with all my heart and wanted to be the dad she deserved, but I was an addict. Looking back, I understand how hard it must have been to have me around back then, but all I knew then was that I was *trying*.

Things turned to war between Kathy and I after she started seeing a dude named Dave. I knew she'd been going on dates or whatever, but before I even realized she was regularly seeing this guy, she'd already moved Jackie in with him.

"You should talk to me first before you move my daughter into another man's house," I said to her, pissed the fuck off. "It's not right. It's fucking disrespectful."

"He's a good guy," Kathy tried to assure me. "I like him a lot."

Turned out she'd met this douchebag while I was in jail, though she swore nothing happened back then. He was several years older, and I think in her mind, he provided a sense of calmness and security that I'd never been able to.

I had Jackie a couple of times a week which was good though, so my plan was to just keep my mouth shut and deal with it. But it was Kathy who started nitpicking things to bitch about when I'd give Jackie back.

"I saw dog hair in the corner of your place," she'd tell me. "You need to clean that up before she comes back." Then it was: "You let Jackie see *Jurassic Park*? That's not a kid's movie!"

It started small like that, then I get a call from her asking if I had any weed. I was selling weed—in addition to the Valium—then, so I told her yes.

"I might be over later to grab some then," she said. "I'll give you a call."

She never called back, and when I got home that afternoon, I saw someone had broken in. There was a trail of weed where I kept mine, so I called Kathy.

"Did you stop here and take some weed?"

"No, I didn't."

"That's weird. I figured it had to be you," I said.

I hung up and left to go pick Jackie up from daycare. When Kathy got there to take Jackie that night, I brought the kid outside to put her in the car seat. Right there in the car, I saw my weed.

"What's this?" I pressed Kathy.

"It's not yours, Joey. Mind your fucking business. I gotta go."

The next day I heard from my attorney saying Kathy wanted me to start getting drug tested for marijuana. Un-fucking-believable.

I got drug tested regularly again from that point on.

One night, two dudes attacked me with fucking two-by-fours. I single-handedly took down both guys (don't fuck with me, Jack!). Afterward, I dropped onto my couch and made a mental list of those who wanted me dead. Kathy and Dave topped the list. They wanted me out of their lives one way or another, and frankly, I wanted to be out of theirs, too.

But I had to keep on trying.

I had two goals at the time: to be a good father and to be a full-time comedian. By now, I had a good grip on what it took to be a comic—just get onstage. Get onstage as much as possible, take your lumps, and get better. I even started to slowly get my own voice up there. I figured one-liners were becoming my thing, and mostly dirty jokes, besides this one I had that was something about Godzilla attacking New York City, but because the air was so polluted, he decided to leave.

So ehhh, who knows if the jokes were good or not, but I knew I was off and running with comedy, if only by way of committing to it. I was out there performing six or seven nights a week. Monday was a club in Boulder; Tuesday was Comedy Works; Wednesday was Club 52; Thursday was El Torito in Denver; on Friday and Saturday I'd do guest sets at different clubs; and Sunday there was an open mic after a line dancing class at some country Western bar, so I'd take advantage of that opportunity, too. None of these places were really any more significant to perform at than the others; these weren't big shows. The maximum audience any of them would get was like forty people, mostly bar regulars and friends of the comics. But it was practice for me and the other local amateur comics, and a few of us would do that same rotation every week with hopes of making it big one day.

I ended up getting a steady gig as an MC at a place called The Broker that had food specials for specific nights of the week, like one night was a prime rib dinner for $15.95. Every night had its own set of regulars I'd perform for who'd come for whatever food special they liked; the food is what really brought people in, not the comedy, but what the hell did I care? It forced me to write new jokes and, to keep things fresh for these people, I'd try wearing different suits or other goofy outfits. I was willing to try any gimmick to get a laugh. Once I even went onstage with no shirt and one of those cone bras Madonna had on in her "Express Yourself" video.

The way I saw it, I just needed to keep showing up, and keep showing up, and eventually somebody would notice. And somebody did.

I got a call saying HBO was doing a traveling show with Carlos Mencia and they wanted me to join him for a couple of the shows. I was over the fucking moon. It was one of the first big-time opportunities for me, so I revisited every joke I'd written in my notebooks to see which ones would hit hardest. I put together a set and rehearsed it on any stage I could. Then, when I got to Mencia's shows, people liked what I did up there—they were laughing their asses off.

Meanwhile, Kathy (and Dave) had no mercy on me whatsoever. I decided to stay on the high road and remained a total gentleman and polite no matter what she tried to blame me for. I kept it simple with them. Hellos, goodbyes, how are yous, and that's it. No tough guy shit.

But my attorney bills were coming one after the other, completely wiping me out every time I'd get ahead. One month I made sixty thousand at the sports betting job I had, and I was still fucking broke. Every time I even picked up the phone to talk to the lawyer it was two hundred bucks.

I tried my hardest to stay positive. Every night I'd write down my comedy goals to wish it all into existence. This included people I wanted to eventually perform with, like Doug Stanhope and Rick Ducommun. There was one comedy newspaper called *Just For Laughs* that would feature all of the top clubs in the country, and I'd go through it every night and circle clubs I wanted to perform at, like The Comedy Store in Los Angeles. It was the home of the greats. I wanted to be onstage there more than I wanted to fucking breathe.

———

I continued to mind my own business and play nice with Kathy and Dave, but they refused to let up. By the holidays the next year, they continued pushing drug abuse allegations on me to keep me away from Jackie. When I got word from my attorney that I wouldn't be getting Jackie at all for the holidays, after a year of being patient, I fucking lost it.

I ran to a buddy's house down the street, knocked on the door, and his wife answered.

"I'm sorry to bother you, but I have a piece of meat I want to cut up and my ex-wife took all of my cutlery," I told her. "Any chance I can borrow a big knife?"

She didn't think twice and handed over a giant kitchen knife. I got in my car and drove to Dave's office. It was fucking over. I'd already decided. I was going to stab this guy to death, get life in prison, then have my friends give me money for a fax machine so I could fax jokes from prison to Jay Leno at *The Tonight Show*. That was my plan.

"I'm not putting up with this shit anymore!" I screamed out loud to myself the entire drive there. When I got to his office building, I stuck the knife under my shirt and walked inside—booking it right past the receptionist. I got in the elevator, determined.

"Good morning," a woman sitting at a desk on Dave's floor said to me. "Can I help you with something?'

"Is Dave here? I'm a buddy of his."

"Dave went out for lunch. He took an early lunch today . . ."

I must have blacked out from anger, because next thing I know a security officer was guiding me back out of the building.

"Sorry, sir, you can't be in here," he told me. "We'll have your friend give you a call when he gets back. What's your name?"

I said nothing. I got back into the elevator and reversed my steps back to my car. As soon as I got in, I broke down. I cried like a child. These assholes had driven me to actually want to kill a man. I still believe I would have stabbed Dave if he'd been there. I wiped my face and promised myself that I'd never let Kathy and Dave fuck with me again.

I called my attorney when I got home.

"Listen, call them back and tell them this is not acceptable," I said. "Tell them I'm taking them to court after the holidays."

The next morning, scared shitless, they dropped Jackie off for Christmas.

With no money for gifts, I'd stolen a bunch of expensive shit from Toys "R" Us, then returned it for a ton of store credit to get Jackie presents she'd like, including a bike. I had my friends from the local Chinese restaurant float me some food so we could have a nice dinner, and I went down to a tree spot near me to plead with the guy to let me have a little tree, at least. When I got there, the guy was MIA and there was a sign hanging up that said: *If you take a tree, rip off the sticker and leave the sticker & cash in the envelope.*

"Is this guy fucking serious?" I said, snatching the three hundred bucks in the envelope and grabbing a tree of my choice. (I did leave an IOU for the tree and signed my name, though, swear to God.)

I had a real cute little one-bedroom apartment then, fit for a bachelor, that was only four hundred bucks a month. The bed in there was so big you couldn't even walk into the bedroom; it took up the entire room. In the living room, I had a little couch and a weightlifting bench that doubled as a coffee table and footrest. I had a dinner table and a TV—and that's all I owned. For Christmas, I decorated every inch. The smile on Jackie's face was priceless. We had the best Christmas together, opening presents and watching *Beauty and the Beast*.

Right after the holidays, Kathy and Dave were back at it. One day during a handoff Kathy was being rude to me and tossing out insults. I told her to go fuck herself. A week later, my attorney called again and said she had filed a motion that she was scared I was going to kidnap Jackie.

From then on, we needed a court-appointed person to serve as the drop off in-between. That lasted four weeks before Dave somehow got that job. I started realizing I would never be given a real chance to raise this child. My patience was running thin, but again, looking back I can see how some of my behavior—including my drug use—played into the way they treated me. Anyway, it all came to a head one day when I was driving with Jackie to meet Dave for the drop off.

"Daddy, what does spic mean?"

I couldn't believe what I was hearing. "Why do you want to know?"

Honestly, the word doesn't bother me. I grew up in Jersey in the '70s; that's just what I was called out there. But my kid was four years old and had lived in Boulder her whole life. How would she ever hear that word? She didn't even look Spanish.

"Every time you call the house, Dave calls you that."

I pulled into the Safeway parking lot and told her to stay in the car while I went right up to Dave.

"Listen. I just need to know. Did you say 'spic' when I called the house?"

He got all flustered and said he was going to call the police. If he was going to get the cops involved, I was going to give him a reason. I hit him twice, right in the fucking face. Once again, I was ready to go back to prison if it meant taking this fucker out.

When the cops showed up, one of them was a guy I'd bonded with when I did my community service at the HIV/AIDS center years back as James Smith. He'd been a security guard there. I was sure I'd be arrested—this was assault, and I had felonies—but instead, he just wrote us both tickets and told us to go to court.

For years after I'd gotten out of jail, I wrote letters to the judge who'd sentenced me to keep him updated on my life and thank him for giving me a second chance. He'd moved over to civil court, and when Dave and I showed up for our case, he was the judge. He threw the entire case against me out of court.

Outside of the courthouse, I unleashed on Kathy. I'd been patient enough, and now I let her have it.

"You've been trying to cut my legs off for four fucking years, and I did nothing to you!" When I say I was screaming, I was *screaming*. "Hey, have you ever told Dave how much you love getting carrots shoved up your ass? Have you? Dave, did you know that?"

I'd never personally put a carrot in her ass, but I had to say *something*.

I kept yelling, going completely over the top. All I kept thinking to myself was: "This is a fucking joke. It's a three-ring circus."

I left that day knowing damn well this was the end. This wasn't any way to live—for me, for them, or for Jackie.

Jackie was becoming more impressionable, and whatever those douchebags were telling her at their house was seeping into her mind. One day she sped away from me on her bike, and when I finally caught up, she spit in my face. She was starting to hate me; I knew this situation was not making this kid happy. She was confused, and they were not going to let me be her dad, no matter how hard I tried. It was as if they were dropping her off to a babysitter when they left her with me, and one they barely trusted at that. They didn't let me be a father—that's the truth.

I was thirty-three years old, still doing cocaine, living paycheck to paycheck, and unstable. I wanted to be a father so bad, but that didn't necessarily mean I *was* a father. I started doing some soul searching. What was really right for this kid? Would things get better, or would they continue to get worse?

I knew it was not going to end well if I stayed. It wasn't a decision I took lightly. It ate away at me. All I wanted was what was best for Jackie, and I knew this situation wasn't that. I knew Kathy would do whatever she could to make my life a living hell, in turn making *all* our lives a living hell, Jackie's most importantly. I started considering what it would be like if I left—and where I would go. I'd met a girl named Devin at one of my gigs, and she was living in Seattle. I got to thinking about Seattle, since I knew the comedy scene there was tremendous and it would be a good place for me to improve my game. I wasn't intending to leave forever. In fact, when I talked to Kathy about it, I told her I'd be gone for a couple of months, tops. But in my heart of hearts, I knew if I left, I was never coming back.

The last time I saw Jackie, she knew what was happening. She knew I was hitting the road to be a comedian and we hugged. She was sad and I was sad. I was fucking heartbroken to leave her, but I knew it was the right thing to do. This kid didn't deserve to grow up around the chaos that was my life, and particularly my life with Kathy and Dave in it. Jackie deserved a life of normalcy—no fighting, nothing like that. She deserved the right kind of childhood, and the only way she was going to get that was if I disappeared.

19

Fat Baby

The first time I went to Comedy Underground in Seattle, I remember staring up at it in awe. This club was a staple in the Pacific Northwest. As I stood there, a weight lifted off my shoulders just thinking of the opportunities this place could bring me. It made the sting of leaving Jackie lessen, at least a little.

In Seattle I ran into this young guy in a backwards Red Sox hat named Josh Wolf. I was happy to find another East Coast guy, and he broke down the local scene for me. Seattle had comedy all over the place. I started getting onstage twice a night, seven nights a week, performing with Josh and other fellow up-and-comers Mitch Hedberg and Brody Stevens. I wasn't doing great, at first. I was bombing a lot—I'd get up there and say some dirty shit most of the crowd hated, or my jokes wouldn't string together right, and I'd be a little too fucked up—but I was putting in the time to get better, taking every chance to practice.

I even played a gay bar where I had to perform in a cage. It got to the point where I was taking so many of the local spots that another comic threatened to beat me up, but I let it go.

Yeah, I was a dirty comic, which meant I'd always be an outsider in this game, but despite that, I was invited to perform at the prestigious Seattle Comedy Competition. There were a ton of great comics in this competition, about sixty of us total, and I ended up placing sixth—right behind Aisha Tylor—which was a tremendous feather in my cap.

One night I was doing a show at Comedy Underground, and when I got offstage, a guy came up to me and asked if I'd ever taken acting lessons.

"I think you could be a natural actor," he said. "You've got something about you, man."

"You think?" I asked, shocked. "I've never acted."

"I have a pilot I'm working on for CBS, and honestly, you're perfect for the role."

He gave me his contact information and asked me to send him an audition tape. He was based out in Los Angeles, which seemed like a cool spot, so I sent a tape and he and I stayed in touch.

Then, Doug Stanhope came to town. I'd seen him perform a while back and he was so good and so free onstage that I cried myself to sleep that night. I remember I cancelled my show the next day and thought about quitting comedy for good. I could never be that funny. Now, almost a year later, he was the hottest comic in the country, and turns out he wanted me to open for him.

"I heard the big guy from Boulder got funny," he said to me.

I wanted to *be* this guy. He was a comedy idol, and now I was getting to open for him. It was a goal coming to life.

After the show, Stanhope asked me when I was moving to LA.

"Fuck no, never. I'm not good enough for that," I said.

"Dude, you're perfect for LA. They're ready for you and your comedy out there, trust me. And there's a huge Latino movement happening there, too."

"I've only been doing comedy a few years . . ."

"Why would I fuck with you?" he asked. "You're better than half the people out there right now. Anyway, if you decide to come out there, call me."

This guy believed what he was telling me, and suddenly, I started to believe it too.

―――――――

It felt like stars were aligning when I got a callback about the pilot right after the Stanhope conversation; the pilot was a go, and they wanted me. I needed to be out in LA and ready to film it in a few weeks.

In late January of 1997, I started the drive to Los Angeles. Devin, my girlfriend from Seattle, came with me, too. She and I had a very hot and cold relationship, but right then we were *hot*, and we were ready to take LA by the balls, even if I was a little nervous at first.

If someone asked me where I'd be by my mid-thirties, I would have said back in jail or dead. I didn't think I deserved success after all the bad shit I'd done. Instead, here I was, off to one of the biggest cities in the country for comedy, and fuck yeah, I felt insecure about it. This was the major leagues, and I was no major leaguer. I had a serious criminal record for fuck's sake. Then something happened on the way to the dance. I read about Tim Allen and how he'd gone to prison for coke. At the time I read that article, Tim Allen was the fucking king of television. He was on ABC, a network owned by Disney of all things, even though he'd been a convicted cocaine dealer. Maybe I *could* do this. I decided my best bet was to keep my fucking mouth shut. No one needed to know about my past. If they found out, so be it, but I wasn't going to give up the information freely.

Turns out, LA was the move that propelled me to where I am today. When we arrived in Hollywood, Devin and I pulled onto a block—Fairfax and Hollywood Boulevard. We headed to a restaurant called Acapulco, an all-you-can-eat Mexican spot. Afterwards, we hit The Comedy Store. The Comedy Store was a comic's dream, especially mine. The Comedy Store was where any comic who cared about comedy wanted to be. It's where my heroes like Richard Pryor, Andrew Dice Clay, and Sam Kinison cut their teeth. Standing there, I was like a kid in a candy store. The first person I saw was Eddie Griffin.

"I'm a big fan." I walked right up to him, sticking out my hand to shake his. "A really big fan. I'm Joey."

"Joey, nice to meet you." He shook my hand.

"I'm a comic, well trying to be," I explained. "It's crazy to walk in here and see guys like you."

"You're trying to be a comic? Well, this is the right fucking place."

We talked a little more and he introduced me to a guy named Don Barris. Before I knew it, Don was putting me up onstage for a three-minute spot that very night. I shook out my nerves and went for it: *"So I've been thinking about killing my ex-wife . . ."*

It went fucking great. People were laughing the whole time. Performing that first time at The Comedy Store felt like even more of a rush than what I felt the first time I *ever* performed back at Comedy Works. I just performed at the motherfucking Comedy Store—and I did *good.* Any fear of not being able to cover the spread had gone away. I felt welcome in this fucking town, and I was ready to accept the challenge of finding my way here. I had a feeling after that set that LA would be home for me for a long, long time, and it was.

I thought back to those nights in Colorado when I'd be writing down my goals and circling comedy club names in the newspaper—this was it. I was living those dreams.

After the show, we hung around The Store for another fifteen minutes, but then I had to get out of there and process what happened. As we were leaving, someone suggested I give it a go for The Laugh Factory's open mic. It was one of those things where I had to show up at 8 AM and I'd be given a number. I'd wait all day to see if they'd call my number, and if they did, I'd get a shot to perform some of my jokes. If the guy from The Laugh Factory liked me, I'd get a showcase for his club. A showcase is what people would consider a typical comedy set, where a place books a comedian in advance because of their skill, name, or both.

I wanted to be a regular at The Comedy Store, but I had heard of that taking years for some people, so I set my sights on The Laugh Factory first. I went there the next morning not realizing I was about to be a victim of the Hollywood power game. There were a ton of other aspiring comics waiting there, like thirty or forty other comics besides me, and we had to stand there for the entire day outside in the heat to see if they called our numbers. It was cool, though, because the seasoned, big comics would often do these guys a solid by driving by and bringing them waters and bagels and shit. I liked hearing that most comics were really trying to just help each other out.

I learned two valuable lessons that day, sweating my dick off and waiting for my number to be called. The first is that I'd fallen into that power struggle, and if I wanted to try to make it here, I had to get used to it. The second thing was how to carry myself as a comedian. That meant shutting my fucking mouth. In Jersey, we always knew to keep our mouths shut and our ears open: to watch, listen, and learn. I knew back then that nobody wants to hear what the fuck you had to say. Here it was more of the same. That first day, there was a big loud guy, so fucking obnoxious. This guy didn't shut up for the entire day. He seemed to know everyone and he was acting like the authority there. I had no idea who he was, but his voice was piercing through me for hours.

When my number finally got called, I got to do three minutes—and I mean, three minutes maximum. At that mark, a guy on a piano started playing as a cue to shut the fuck up. I was happy with what I did up there. I kept it dirty, some filthy shit about my sex life that I thought people could relate to. Let's say there were about twenty people listening in the audience. I think I got all of them laughing for most of my three minutes. I had to wait until everyone else was done before I'd be able to get any feedback on whether I'd have a date to come back and showcase.

Waiting again, I heard them call the big guy up. I had to fucking see this, because this guy was the authority on comedy, you know? He got onstage, and his voice disappeared. He sounded like a fucking mouse. It was hilarious.

When they called my name again, I was feeling pretty good.

"Why are you here?" the dude asked me.

"Well, I'm trying to be a comic," I said.

"You're not a comic. You're a nightclub act."

I looked at him, not saying a word.

"My recommendation is that you move to Vegas and do nightclubs," he continued, looking down at his notebook, then back up to me. "You aren't fit to be a LA comic. But, good luck."

I was in shock. I left there fucking mummified. I figured I was done. I called Stanhope and gave him the scoop.

"That guy is a fucking idiot," he said. "Look at the people he has performing in that place right now. You don't want to be in there anyway. You're a smart guy, Coco, and a great fucking comic."

Remembering how well my Comedy Store set went and Stanhope's encouraging words, I decided to stay strong. Becoming a regular at The Store only depended on one thing: If Mitzi Shore thought you were funny or not. Mitzi was the longtime owner of The Store, and her word was gold. If I was able to showcase for her, and she liked me, I'd be set. But it was tough to get in front of her. Every manager in town was trying to get their comic in there. Plus, if you showcased for Mitzi and she didn't like you, you were done. I figured for me though, it was worth a shot.

"What do you think?" I asked Stanhope. "Think you can get me a showcase?"

Stanhope called over there for me and so did Carlos Mencia. I'd also gotten to meet and know one of my other comedy idols (and someone I hoped to work with as part of my comedy goals written back in Colorado), Rick Ducommun, and he called for me, too.

Then, the phone rang on my end.

"Is this, uh . . . Joey 'Coco' Diaz?" a guy asked.

"Yeah, this is Coco."

"I'm the booker down at The Comedy Store, and hey, I've been hearing a lot about you," he said. "A bunch of comics are telling me I need to get you in here to showcase. So I'm going to put you on the list."

"Are you fucking serious?"

"It's going to take six to eight months or so for us to get you in, but we're going to make it happen. I'm adding you to the list right now."

"Thank you so much. I can't tell you how much I appreciate this. I'll be ready."

I wasn't kidding. I committed myself to continuing to grow my comedy skill while I waited.

Meanwhile, to bring in money, I took a job selling cigars over the phone. Cigars were fucking big back then. Everywhere was selling the things, and everywhere people were smoking them. I was making somewhere near nine hundred a week just doing this for a few hours in the mornings. Then at night, I practiced my comedy.

I went to coffee shops, improvs, bars . . . anywhere with a mic that would let me get a few minutes with an audience. If a joke fell flat, I wouldn't fucking use it again. If a joke hit, I would bring it back to another audience but tweaked to see if it would do better or worse. I kept notes on all of it. I also would hang round The Store constantly just so people got used to seeing me. I wasn't getting paid for any of my comedy, but I was still rocking and rolling.

Then, after only a few weeks of the grind, the news came that I'd been waiting for—The Store was ready for me; I had my showcase locked up. I grabbed my notebook and put together the best three-minute set I could possibly come up with based on everything I'd practiced in LA. The night of my showcase, Eddie Griffin did me a solid by sitting next to Mitzi and making sure no one tried to talk to her during my set. We wanted her fully focused.

I never felt so fucking nervous. I had to pump myself up in the bathroom beforehand, staring at myself in the mirror, saying, "You fucking got this, Joey! You fucking *got this*!" I knew if I bombed here, in front of Mitzi, I'd be packing up and heading back to Boulder and giving up on this dream. Or more likely, I'd go back to North Bergen and snort coke until I fucking died. This was my big chance; I couldn't fuck this up.

"Joey 'Coco' Diaz!" When I heard them announce my name, I went into a trance. Much like my first time at Comedy Works, I couldn't even tell you what I said—I blacked out—all I know is that I heard nonstop laughter, and it fueled me. When I got offstage, I walked up to Mitzi and sincerely thanked her for the showcase. "I really appreciate you letting me get up there. It's an honor."

"Can you do ten minutes?" Mitzi asked.

"Huh?"

"Ten minutes . . . can you do a ten-minute set?" she asked again.

"Yes, yes, definitely . . ."

"I'll see you next Sunday, then."

It was a fucking godsend. Mitzi Shore liked my comedy. When I got home, I took my notebook out and immediately started putting together a ten-minute set, using all of my best material, and a quick, filthy story about some lady I'd fucked back in Colorado who only had one leg. Ultimately, I put together a set that had plenty of dirty shit in it, but fuck if that wasn't me.

The next Sunday, on my thirty-fourth birthday, I headed back to The Comedy Store. My anxiety was so high that I wanted to cry—but it was a different type of anxiety. It felt . . . better. I had something to look forward to. I got up on that stage to do my ten-minute set and gave it everything I had.

"Cocaine will make you do some crazy shit . . ."

I held nothing back. All the pain I'd experienced throughout my life, I channeled it all into making this the best set possible. And I fucking killed it. When I came offstage, Mitzi looked at me, nodded, and said, "Congratulations, you're a regular." I couldn't believe my ears.

"You're funny," she added. "Hey, you should wear a diaper and call yourself 'Fat Baby.'"

Hah! Not all of Mitzi's ideas were gold, but I was just fucking excited to get the gig.

To say The Comedy Store changed my life wouldn't be giving it enough credit. That place was *it* for my professional life—and soon enough, my love life, too. The Store gave me the confidence boost I needed. Anyone who was anyone in comedy in LA was performing there, and I was welcomed with open arms. I became a student of the game, studying what these other comics were doing, showing up every chance I could to watch them and take notes. I loved comedy before, but now I was *really* in love with comedy. I held onto it with kid gloves. I respected comedy like a fucking religion.

———

I told every club owner in LA who would listen that I was available wherever they wanted me while I was preparing to shoot my pilot. The show was going to be called *Bronx County*, and it was supposed to be CBS's answer to *NYPD Blue*. All of us on the production thought it would be a huge hit. Unfortunately, we were wrong. It didn't even get picked up.

I was bummed but, truthfully, being on that set showed me I had no fucking idea what I was doing as an actor. The problem with my acting career was simple: I had no experience. Like, zero. I was totally green. I remember the first day they told me to get on my mark, and I didn't know what the fuck that meant. We were running a race? I thought we were filming a show.

Everyone was looking at me fucking weird. A few days in, they started treating me differently, too. I could tell there was a problem. They kept shortening my lines little by little until the original four pages of dialog for my character, a bartender in the show, were cut down to about two lines total.

I needed to learn the basics if I wanted to add acting to my resume. I joined a local acting class and found myself an agent who started sending me out on commercial auditions. I was too embarrassed to let anyone know I had no clue how to act, so I didn't say dick and just kept showing up, giving it my best, like I'd done with comedy.

I even ended up in a Scientology acting class. It was a free class, which was great, but at the end of every class they'd beat you up to join Scientology. If an hour was spent on acting lessons, the next hour was spent trying to fend the teachers off. Fuck if these guys thought they could rope me in. When they made me fill out a questionnaire if I wanted to keep coming back, I marked it with all false answers. Sexual orientation: gay, that kind of shit. I never went back.

That Fourth of July weekend, after being in LA for a few months, I landed my first national commercial with Taco Bell. To be honest, I'm not really sure why they wanted me—maybe I just fit the image of a Taco Bell eater, but my acting was still brutal. They were planning to shoot three commercials in three days, but when I got there, I found out my commercial was cut before we even started shooting. They told me to stick around set, just in case they had a spot to squeeze me in.

One of the days on set, a bunch of us—including the director—were having lunch together.

"Hey," he pulled me aside afterwards. "You had me dying laughing at lunch today. Stay close to me, and I'm going to try to get you into one of these."

And he did. I made it in, sitting there getting my shoes shined as the Taco Bell chihuahua ran by. It was cool to see myself on TV, but the money from this thing . . . holy fuck. The first check alone was twenty grand, and the checks kept coming. I couldn't cash these things fast enough before the next one came. I was able to pay down my debts, but the money also fueled my cocaine habit, which had come with me to LA.

I was back to doing blow seven nights a week. This time, though, I'd made peace with my drug use. Instead of giving myself constant grief about it—quitting, then starting again, an endless cycle—I was just *going for it*. I wasn't going to live my life yes-ing and no-ing myself. I was committing to coke. The way my addict mind saw it, there was no way cocaine would affect my comedy for the worse. I was killing it.

20

Love and Comedy

One of the first friends I made in comedy in Los Angeles was a dude by the name of Joe Rogan; we hit it off right off the bat. Joe was never a criminal, never a drug addict—hell, the guy never even really drank. I had no fucking idea why he wanted to hang out with me. I guess it was our mutual respect for comedy that brought us together.

Joe would come into The Store a lot, and they'd bring him up as the guy from *NewsRadio*. One night after our sets, we started talking, and I told him how interested I was in TV.

"Any chance I could come watch one of the *NewsRadio* tapings?" I asked him.

"Absolutely. I'll get you tickets," he told me.

I'd never watched a show being filmed live like that, and it blew me the fuck away. I sat in the audience the first time I went, but the second time, Joe had me come to his trailer and hang backstage with every-one. I was a starving comic—that Taco Bell money was evaporating, unsurprisingly—and being on that set I was shocked to see the amount of food they had. I was used to a cheap lunch: a 99-cent Wendy's burger, a 99-cent bowl of chili, and a soda. When I saw the spread they had backstage at *NewsRadio*, I had to go in for the kill. I went up and started eating the crackers and stuff like that. Then, I saw a platter of jumbo shrimp. I stood there eating and eating and eating.

"You had me laughing all day today," Joe said to me later. "You in that leather jacket. People were terrified of you; they kept asking about the scary guy eating all the shrimp. I fucking loved it."

A normal celebrity would have been embarrassed to have me there, fingers still sticky with cocktail sauce, but Joe wasn't that kind of guy. He thought it was funny and invited me back.

I loved getting to hang out with Joe because his work ethic really inspired me. This guy was busting his ass, and no matter how big he was getting, how much money he was making, or how little time he had, he'd always make it to The Store for his fifteen-dollar set on a Friday night. I also loved Joe because he was honest; he kept it real. I was onstage bomb-ing one night during a fifteen-minute set at The Store—jokes I hadn't spent enough time working through weren't making sense to the audience, and it was crickets—so I eventually said to the crowd, "You're killing me."

From the back, I heard Joe scream, "No, *you're* killing *me!*"

That alone gave me the motivation to bring my A game there every time moving forward; to pretend every time was my first time there. This was the world-famous Comedy Store, and I was lucky to have the opportunity.

Another person I became quick friends with there was Marilyn Martinez, another regular at The Store. I loved Marilyn because she didn't give a fuck what anyone thought. Her comedy was dirty, and she was unapologetic about it. She inspired me to continue to have a *fuck it* way of telling my jokes and stories onstage.

Thankfully I was making friends, because my living situation was fluid as fuck in LA in the beginning, and I needed to lean on my buddies here and there. As I said, I'd first moved there with Devin a couple of years prior. Let me tell you a little more about Devin—she was a stripper, originally from Michigan, who looked like Kelly LeBrock from the movie *Weird Science*. She was beautiful, sweet, and off-the-chain smart. She had a lot of layers, this girl. She had a crazy upbringing—one that isn't my place to tell—and it affected her adult life in countless ways, like my childhood had affected mine.

Back then and throughout the years since, Devin would always have men all over the country willing to pay her for all kinds of shit, like twenty-five grand to light her pussy on fire, that kind of stuff. Devin was—and still is—a sexual boss bitch, and I love her for it to this day.

When I first met Devin, she was having boyfriend trouble, so we stayed up all night and talked about it, smoked pot, and giggled a little. I knew right away she was a bad egg, I could just smell it, but we became friends. Eventually, Devin ditched that boyfriend and she and I started dating, but there was still one little problem: Devin also had a sugar daddy. He and I only fought once, but having him in the picture was definitely inconvenient.

One of the best things about Devin was that she supported my comedy, no matter what. She was my biggest fan, always showing up to any show she could, and laughing at even my worst material. And there was so much fucking passion with Devin, too. Like I said earlier, when things were hot, they were fucking *hot*.

But when things were not, they were *not*.

We fought non-fucking-stop, and over time—especially when we hit LA—our bad moments started outweighing our good ones. We got into a habit of breaking up, getting back together two weeks later, then breaking up again. I knew it was time to be single but couldn't seem to separate myself from her. Devin and I were too awful together to remain a couple. I just needed a final reason to end it.

A friend of a friend who was out of the country had given me their car to drive around for a while in LA, but when the registration expired and there was no way to renew it, I kept getting tickets. The tickets started mounting up. Meanwhile, I was living out of that car part-time, sometimes crashing with Stanhope or Josh Wolf, who was now also living in LA. Sometimes I was staying in a hotel, and sometimes—if Devin and I were in a good place—I'd crash with her.

On the last day of mine and Devin's relationship, we got into a fight, and when I stormed out of her place, I saw that the car—which had everything I owned in it, clothes, headshots, comedy videotapes, boxing gloves—was towed. That pile of tickets finally caught up to me. All I had were the clothes on my back, so I needed to go get this car back.

I went back inside and asked Devin to give me a ride down to the impound lot in Hollywood. The guy there wouldn't let me get into the car without the registration, so I was fucked. He wouldn't budge, and I wasn't able to get the car back (ever), so I was fuming. Devin and I had just gone grocery shopping before I realized the car was towed, and we had the groceries in Devin's car still—including a pot roast and potatoes. Leaving the impound lot, she and I were screaming at each other. We were fighting so bad on our drive back to her place that Devin pulled over and we both got out, continuing to yell. I don't even remember exactly what we were fighting about—I'm assuming everything and nothing at all.

I just remember grabbing the pot roast and I was going to throw it, at the same time she pulled out mace and was about to spray me.

Standing in the middle of the street with my hands full of pot roast, I knew we were done this time, for good.

Not long after, I started crashing in an apartment building at 1400 North Gardner. It was a little three-story place with about twelve apartments total. Stanhope lived there and tons of other comics I'd become friends with. It was 1999, and this area of the city was the heart and soul of Hollywood then. This was Old Hollywood. Right up the street was the florist where Joe DiMaggio used to buy flowers for Marilyn Monroe, and there was the iconic Guitar Center and The Sunset Grill, all within walking distance.

In a few-block radius there were also the Hollywood Vista Apartments and Sierra Vista apartment complexes, which were big spots for comics to live, too. There was Josh, Mitch Hedberg, Nick Di Paolo, Sean Rouse, and Ralphie May. I moved in with Ralphie at Gardner, and it was fucking tremendous. Me, him, and two other comics lived in the same one-bedroom, with Ralphie in the bed—he must have been six hundred pounds at the time—and the rest of us crashing on the floor.

Those were some of the best days of my life. Gardner was right behind a well-known bar called El Compadre. It's a Mexican joint that was always packed, and it was a fucking party. At one point, our friends were taking up at least half of the apartments at Gardner. One girl was a producer on a reality show, another was a writer on another show, another friend of ours played violin. Everybody was in the entertainment business, and we were all young and just getting started. We were all out of control. It was the perfect little scene.

Next to Gardner was a strip of little houses, and behind that was a parking garage where famous people would park their cars. Matthew McConaughey lived in that neighborhood when he was a struggling actor. When he blew up, he moved to Hollywood Hills but kept his car parked in the garage down by us.

One day I walked into our apartment and saw Ralphie on the floor looking out the window.

"Yo, what the fuck are you doing?" I asked him, laughing.

"I'm torturing Matthew McConaughey."

I looked out the window and saw McConaughey out there in the beating hot sun with no shirt on, fixing his car.

"Watch this," Ralphie said to me. "Matthew McConaughey, you suck!!!" he screamed out the window, ducking back down.

I peeked out and saw McConaughey spin around from his car, searching for where the screams came from. Ralphie went on to do this for a solid hour before McConaughey started losing his mind.

"Hey, Matthew McConaughey . . . I saw *The Wedding Planner,*" Ralphie screamed. "It sucked! You owe me seven-fifty!"

"Alright!" McConaughey screamed back, now pissed as fuck. "Have some balls and come down here and say it to my face."

Ralphie and I were dying laughing. Ralphie kept this up every time he saw McConaughey down there for almost an entire year. After a while of being challenged to come down and face him man-to-man, Ralphie finally took him up on it. When Ralphie got down there and they realized they were both from Texas, instead of fighting they quickly bonded, and they came back up to the apartment and smoked weed together.

As much as there was ball-busting, there was just a lot of love between everyone living there. We did family-style dinners four nights a week. We'd sit around and tell each other stories of shit we'd done in our lives, and just laugh our asses off. I always knew I had wild stories to share with people—I'd been through some shit, you feel me? But when I started telling them as obscenely as possible to my buddies there, leaving them in tears, I felt like I might be onto something with my comedy angle.

I was still broke, but I was doing exactly what I wanted to do with my life and I had fucking tremendous friends, too. You can't put a price tag on that.

———

One night at The Comedy Store, I saw a girl walking down the stairs—a waitress named Terrie who'd apparently been there for a couple of years, too, but who I'd never seen before. This girl was beautiful; her blue eyes lit up the entire room. When I locked eyes with her, I completely froze. I needed to get to know her.

I never expected to fall in love again after the shit that went down with Kathy, then Devin. I'd sort of sworn off the idea of getting too serious with anyone else. I was committed to not being committed. I'd never get married again, and any girl I'd pursue, I'd keep it light.

Then Terrie turned everything upside down. When we met, I had nothing going on in my life besides comedy, but she still gave me a chance. She'd recently turned thirty and had taken a vow to get her act together—to become more established. She'd just gotten herself a new VCR and a cat named Finney to prove to herself that she was an adult. She didn't do drugs; no pot at all. She was just a regular, nice girl from Tennessee who'd moved to LA and was waitressing while she tried her hand at acting. Meanwhile, I was living with a rotation of friends again— and still sometimes sleeping in a car, another one I didn't even own.

The first time I talked to Terrie, her accent got me. I was a goner. Her sweetness just jumped out at me, too. She was different from any girl I'd ever met. I knew I needed to treat this situation differently than I had with other women, so I started slow by asking her out for coffee. Not long after our coffee date, I asked her to lunch. I only had ten bucks on me and no car that day, so I walked about a mile and a half to her place. When I got there and rang the doorbell, I realized—for real—that I had nothing to offer her. I wasn't sure why I was even making the attempt, but I had to try.

"I'm really embarrassed, but I don't know many places we can go out with this," I pulled out the ten-dollar bill from my pocket, showing it to her as I felt my balls shriveling up.

"Come inside," she said without hesitating. "I'll cook us something."

She made me a piece of chicken with red beans, and it was fucking delicious. You know what they say, the way to a man's heart is through his stomach. And she fucking nailed it.

From then on, I was hooked—I couldn't get enough of this sweet girl. Keeping with my more wholesome approach, for the first couple of weeks, I didn't even try anything with her, nothing sexual at all. I wanted her to know I respected her and really cared, and I wanted to honor the fact that she was so nice and deserved a great man.

That summer—the summer of 2000—I had a gig in Lake Havasu City, Arizona, and no way to get out there. When I told Terrie, she offered to drive me. Finney being a new cat and all, she didn't want to leave him home alone. This made me like Terrie even more, and we ended up bringing Finney on the trip with us.

The whole trip was a comedy of errors—from Finney lodging himself beneath the gas pedal while Terrie was driving and us almost crashing, to a broken speedometer, to the top plastic cover of the windshield breaking and flapping while we were driving—it was one thing after another, but we laughed the whole time. I remember looking at her on the drive home and telling myself, "I have to get my act together for this girl."

After the Lake Havasu City trip, Terrie and I were officially a couple without having to really say it, and every day she would impress me more. The way she cared about me was so different from anything I'd experienced as an adult. It was the kind of love I remember having as a kid.

A little while into us dating, I was scheduled to be in NYC for a one-man show. The night before I had to leave, Terrie and I were hanging out.

"Do you have enough money for this trip?" she asked as we were saying our goodbyes. Terrie was also tight on cash then but insanely generous.

"Ehhh, not really, but I'll make it work," I told her.

Right away, she went into her purse and gave me the cash she'd made waitressing the night before. Then she handed me the rest of her cigarettes.

"Here," she said, before giving me a hug. "Have a safe trip."

She meant it as a small gesture, but it stuck with me. Terrie accepted me for who I was—a guy with some deep-seated issues and a questionable past who, deep down, had a good heart. She never asked me to change.

Employees weren't allowed to date at The Store, so we kept our relationship under wraps, but I ended up moving in with her pretty quick, basically just taking my duffle bag of random shit and relocating it permanently to her place. I was thirty-seven years old and didn't possess a single thing of value, until I bought us a TV. I'd gotten five hundred bucks for a gig, and Terrie and I stopped at Kmart and bought a TV that was so big it wouldn't even fit in the trunk. We were both so happy. We still have that TV to this day. I refuse to get rid of it because it was the first thing we got as a couple and it solidified our relationship—and growth—in my eyes.

Terrie knew up front where I stood on marriage, and she never gave me a hard time about it. She knew what I'd gone through with my divorce, how it had torn me apart, and how I wasn't sure I'd ever recover from losing Jackie. And Terrie listened. Not just listened, but *listened*. I felt like I could tell her everything. Well, other than how much I loved cocaine. I kept that close.

Terrie was an innocent girl. I mean, she drank, but like I said, she didn't even smoke pot, let alone fuck with cocaine. I eventually told her about my relationship with marijuana—how it was like a medicine to me—but I refused to let her in on my secret coke habit. When we'd be out together, she would be drinking and wouldn't even notice I was doing it; she'd just assume I was really drunk, too. On occasion she'd ask how all my money from stand-up flew out the window so fast after a gig, but for the most part, she didn't pry.

"Do you know you choke in your sleep?" she asked me one morning, very concerned.

"What do you mean?"

"It's like you stop breathing for a second and make a choking sound. It's scary. I think you might need to get it checked out."

I knew something was seriously up with my health, too, but I still hated doctors and wasn't interested in going through the whole bullshit of it. I was only sleeping like two hours a night, using Tylenol PM when I desperately needed sleep, but it would take like ten of them to knock me out. Meanwhile, I'd spend the rest of the day dozing off everywhere I went. And I was gaining weight at the speed of light. In three months, I put on about forty pounds. Plus, I was smoking cigarettes like an animal, like two to three packs a day. Terrie's couch was covered in burns from me dozing off with a cigarette in my mouth. I was going to light that fucking place on fire. I also wasn't exercising at all. I couldn't even climb three flights of stairs. If Terrie's elevator was out, I'd just stay inside the house until they fixed it. My life was comedy, cocaine, and Coca-Cola.

I knew something needed to change with my health, but it took near-death for it to happen. I had a gig at The Funny Bone in Little Rock, Arkansas, and I was sitting on a couch in my hotel's lobby waiting for my ride to the show. I must have dozed off because I was woken up by some dude tapping me on the shoulder.

"Excuse me, I don't mean to bother you . . ." he started saying as I oriented myself. "I'm a doctor, and I know you don't know me, but I need you to listen to me. If you don't go see a doctor about your sleep apnea, you're going to be dead in about ten days."

"Huh?" I asked, taking the business card he was handing me.

"I was up at the desk, and you were snoring so loud—basically choking to death in your sleep. I needed to come over and wake you up. Sleep apnea is the number one fastest-growing disease. People are dying from it."

I sat there processing what he said, how it aligned to what Terrie had been describing, and how I'd been feeling lately.

"Fuck, am I going to die?" I wondered out loud.

"I can tell by the color of your skin, too—or lack of color," he said. "You need to drink a ton of water right now, no alcohol, and go see a specialist right away. And to answer your question, if you don't get this under control, I suspect that yes, you will die from it."

Once Terrie found out, she made me follow up and drove me to the appointments. I did a sleep study, and they told me I was one of the most severe cases they'd ever seen. Like the doctor back in Little Rock said, I was going to choke to death.

They had to put me on a ton of prescription pills and vitamins, and I needed to start using a sleep apnea machine when I slept every night. I still have to use it to this day. It was some scary shit knowing I could have died at any second. It was a real brush with death, and who would have thought, if I died back then, it wouldn't have been drug-related.

As my condition was starting to improve, I realized something: Terrie cared about me more than I'd even suspected. The concern she showed throughout the whole thing—and how she then made it her mission to take care of me, to make sure I made my doctors' appointments, to bring me to them, to remind me to take my pills, to help me with the fucking machine, to listen to it make noises all night next to her—I was blown the fuck away.

If I didn't know it already, this confirmed that Terrie was an absolute keeper. I wouldn't let go of this girl for the world.

21

Joey Diaz, The Actor

One of my first big acting gigs had been in the 1998 movie *BASEketball*, with Trey Parker and Matt Stone, the creators of *South Park*. My acting was still absolute shit back then. I had trouble remembering lines, still struggled with hitting my marks, and just hadn't had enough practice yet. Plus, by the time I was set to film *BASEketball*, I weighed like three hundred fifty pounds. What I didn't realize was that this role would have me on roller skates. Can you imagine a dude that huge on fucking roller skates? Neither could I . . . not to mention I hadn't roller skated in over twenty years. I figured I'd deal with the problem when it came time for me to actually shoot. Until then, I'd get high in my trailer, watch Jenny McCarthy kickboxing outside, and fuck around on set.

One day I had a pair of skates with me in my bag when I left the set, and I'd stopped at a local thrift shop to buy a shirt. When I reached in my bag to pay and saw the skates, I had an idea.

"Hey, do you guys buy roller skates?" I asked the guy behind the counter.

"I mean, yeah, of course," he said.

"Look, I've got a brand-new pair of skates here," I said, tossing them on the counter. "Never used. They're worth three hundred bucks."

The guy examined them before countering. "I'll give you one-twenty."

"Sold," I said, sticking my hand out for the cash. Easy money.

We had tons of those skates on set—multiples in every size. Within about three weeks, I'd managed to sell this guy almost our entire stock. The production guys were going crazy. They couldn't figure out what the fuck was happening to all the skates.

Five weeks in and still waiting to shoot my part, I figured, fuck it. I went out one night, got high, and didn't get home until around eight in the morning. I had to be on set at 9 AM but figured I could just sleep in the trailer all day like I'd been doing every other day. But, on that day, they told me my scene was up next. My eyes were red as fuck and there was alcohol on my breath and cocaine still running through my veins. But I had to shoot this fucking scene *today*.

I'd sold all of the roller skates in my size, but I somehow squeezed my size ten foot into skates a size and a half too small. I kept falling down during every take, and eventually they told me to just ditch the skates. The entire shoot was a mess—I was never so embarrassed in my life. When we wrapped, I went home and figured there was no way they'd use me in the movie. I'd fucked that up, big time. Six months later, the phone rang and they wanted to know how to spell my name for the credits. I made the cut.

It was the first movie premiere I got to go to, and I went alone, took pictures alone, the whole nine. People were coming up and shaking my hand. It was one of those surreal moments where you're going through the motions, but unlike those terrible surreal moments I had following my mom's death, this now seemed almost too good to be true.

All I kept thinking was: "I'm not even an actor, I'm barely a comic." Yet, here I was.

When *The Sopranos* came out the following year and became a huge hit, it was tremendous because everyone kept mistaking me for Vincent Pastore, the guy who played Big Pussy. I even got a call from Juan one day congratulating me on the role, thinking it was really me. Since I resembled Pastore enough, I kept getting hired for a ton of stuff.

I was now getting tons of practice with acting, and it started making a huge difference in the quality of my skills. I had a rotation of agents who helped me hit a hot streak booking acting gigs. I got roles on *Mad TV* and a bunch of cable commercials. I tried Telemundo and got fired because my Spanish was "too street," but I didn't let it slow my momentum. I knew I was getting better—I didn't struggle with those beginner errors anymore—so I felt confident now.

I joined a cold reading workshop with a guy named Christian Kaplan who was a big-time casting director at Fox. The workshop taught me the importance of not kissing people's asses in the audition but instead figuring out a way to blow up the room in a couple of minutes tops; make them unable to forget you. Between that and the genius of Mitzi Shore who had us work on short, three-minute sets and get to the fucking point, I was killing it with auditions. I booked *18 Wheels of Justice*, a crime drama series on TNN, then booked other shows like *ER*, *Cold Case*, *NYPD Blue*, *Karen Sisco*, and *Law & Order: SVU*. My goal on set for these shows was to bring that same energy I'd brought in the audition and prove who the fuck I was.

I even got to work on an episode of a show called *Arli$$* on HBO with James Coburn. We later did *American Gun* together, too (I played the gun smuggler). I was fucking ecstatic because this guy was an idol to me. He was a great actor, he'd worked with Bruce Lee, *and* he smoked pot. Our scene in that first show should have taken about an hour, but we were talking so much that it took about four hours to shoot. He liked me so much that he was coaching me through the scene.

"You have natural instincts, kid," he said to me as we were wrapping. "If you're taking an acting class, I want you to get out of that class because they're going to ruin your instincts."

I couldn't believe what he was saying. I felt like I was a force to be reckoned with.

"I can't believe I have the balls to ask you this right now, but how was Bruce Lee?" I asked.

We both had tears in our eyes as he told me everything Bruce Lee had done for him and how his own acting had improved so much because of him.

Then, I got introduced to a guy named Harry Basil, a comedian and actor, who was a real sweetheart and had seen me at The Store. The night we met, he asked if I wanted to be in the Rodney Dangerfield movie *Back by Midnight*. A Rodney fucking Dangerfield movie! I auditioned a few days later in front of Basil, a bunch of other people like the casting director and the producers, and Rodney himself.

The role I read for turned out to be cast already, but they were determined to give me a place in the movie, so they told me to show up on set and they'd find something for me, which they did. I was on set for ten days, and every day I had to check in personally with Rodney. I'd have to go to his trailer, and he'd open up the door in a robe and no underwear—balls hanging out that were even bigger than mine.

In the short time I spent on set with him, Rodney gave me a sense of acceptance in the comedy world, even beyond what I'd been getting at

The Store. He told me I was funny. I mean my fucking comedy idol—the guy I studied my whole career—thought *I* had what it took. I felt like the world was my fucking oyster.

Off set, while I'd left *most* of my true criminal habits behind when I'd gotten to LA, I was still doing coke and selling it too. One night my pot dealer asked if I could help a music business dude out who was looking for coke. I agreed and met him for coffee. He told me he was in the area for three months and had someone on his end who needed a regular hookup.

"It's very confidential," he said to me, seriously.

I knew he wasn't fucking around, plus I was always looking for extra cash, so I told him yes. The next day, he bought seventeen grams of coke from me. He started calling me every day asking for the same amount. Turned out, this guy was working for Whitney Houston. After about a month of this, I finally got to meet her, too.

"Hey, we're going to be at the recording studio tonight," the guy told me. "Whitney would like you to stop by and say hello. She really likes your coke."

I blew them off—I didn't want to be *that guy*—but within a week he had us officially meet anyway. In real life, Whitney was just as beautiful as you would imagine. As much as she was this extraordinary talent, not even comparable to anyone else, and sweet as could be, she was just a person addicted to cocaine, like I was.

By the time of the Grammys that year, she was up to an 8 ball per day. They'd stocked up for the weekend in advance, but that Monday morning at 9 AM my phone rang.

"Hey, I need to see you today," the guy said.

"Okay, yeah, sure . . . how's like noon?"

"How about now?"

I could tell they were in need.

Forty-five minutes later, a fucking limo rolled up. I got in, and inside were Whitney Houston and Bobby Brown, blasted out of their minds. It was the last time I dealt coke to her, but holy shit I will never forget it.

Back at acting, I'd gotten connected with Georgianne Walken, *The Sopranos* casting director, who had lots of important people in her circles. She'd passed my audition tape on to a colleague of hers, and out of nowhere, I got asked to read for a role in the Robert De Niro movie *Analyze That*. I fucking got it.

Harold Ramis was directing the movie, and I loved that guy. I knew that it didn't matter how small my role was, I'd be lucky enough to just be on this set. It had become my curse that I'd get booked for roles in the opening scene of movies, with credits rolling through me. In this case, I was set to die in the first scene. We ended up shooting in Kearny, New Jersey, at the bar down the street from where I'd gone to school at Sacred Heart School for Boys. I remembered that bar well; it was where the nuns used to go to drink when they weren't kicking the shit out of us at school.

I didn't get to work with De Niro one-on-one on set, but seeing him from a distance was worth it. The best part of that whole experience was a conversation I had with Harold.

"I've been trying to get into the Montreal Comedy Festival, but they still haven't picked me and they're always giving me excuses," I explained to him one day when we were chit-chatting between scenes.

"Just keep doing what you're doing," he told me. "You're a funny guy. Anyone who doesn't see that right away, tell them to go fuck themselves."

I couldn't believe the support he was giving me.

"When I first started, all of my friends were getting hired but everyone was set against me and my work," Harold continued. "So what did I do? I went on to write three of the greatest scripts of all time, and they could choke on them. So fuck 'em. Keep it up."

When I left that set, I was floating in the clouds.

Spider-Man 2 came next. The day of my audition it must have been fucking eighty degrees. I was wearing sweatpants and a sweatshirt and had to walk like two miles to the studio because parking was so overflowed with other people auditioning. I was sweating profusely. I didn't think I'd get the role—this was going to be a huge movie and they wanted Bill Goldberg, not a fat Cuban—but I made an impression with an over-the-top audition where I shocked everyone by knocking over a couch. They were all laughing their asses off and they ended up hiring me.

They told me I'd only be on set for a day, but I ended up being there for over two weeks, and it was tremendous. My first day on set seeing Tobey Maguire, I almost shit myself. I walked around all day watching people, while grabbing fistfuls of food here and there and bottles of pomegranate juice. On Fridays, there was surf and turf, and I would sit there and eat like fifteen lobster tails like a fucking savage.

My closest friend on the set became a twelve-year-old girl in the movie's train scene with me. She would stand there and insult people all day, telling them they were bad actors. She was really a firecracker. One morning, when I was stealing a gallon of pomegranate juice, a dude came up to me.

"What type of influence are you having on my daughter?" the guy asked.

"Uhhh . . . what do you mean?"

He started laughing. "I'm messing with you, man. She came home last week and cracked like a thousand jokes you told her. It was hysterical."

I started laughing too. "Yeah, she's a funny kid. She's a great actress."

"Do you smell marijuana?" he asked, looking around.

"Sorry, yeah, I have some on me," I admitted. "I'm not shooting today so . . ."

"Let's smoke it," he said. It was 7 AM and, fuck yeah, I was on board.

He and I made it a regular thing for the rest of our mornings there; we made the set of *Spider-Man 2* like Cheech and Chong's house. People would walk by us like, "Who is smoking weed this early in the morning?" and we'd just laugh.

"It's disgusting is what it is!" I'd shout back, shaking my head. "Absolutely sick!"

———

I came to understand that in LA it was a numbers game. If I kept pushing, my big break in the acting world would come, and I'd end my opening-credits curse. When I booked *Taxi*, the Queen Latifah movie, I thought that could be it. But when I once again only made it into the opening scene, I knew I needed to keep playing the numbers.

And then my big break happened . . . or so I thought.

I'd seen *The Longest Yard* at the movie theater in Union City when I was a kid. My friends and I were on our feet cheering the whole time, and when Burt Reynolds scored a touchdown, the entire place erupted. I could live to be a hundred and never forget that. So when I heard Adam Sandler was doing a remake, I wanted in. I learned about a part in the film that would be a good fit for me, but word was that they wanted a big name for it—someone like Tony Siragusa or Vincent Pastore. But, I had a plan to get this fucking part.

I was in Houston one weekend doing shows and it came to me: I'd send in a ridiculous video to get their attention. I went out and bought a football shirt, two sizes too small, and a football helmet that was way too small too, and I got one of my friends to help me film. We taped a bunch of stuff, like people throwing the ball to me with my gut hanging out—weighing in at nearly four hundred pounds by then—and the shirt busting at the seams. I mean, it didn't look *flattering*, but it was funny as fuck.

We sent it off to Adam's office and, within days, I got a call for an audition. The audition was going to be just me and the director, a guy named Peter Segal. It went well, but when a month passed with no word, my hopes weren't too high. Then, I got a call from Adam's office saying a few of them wanted to meet me at The Four Seasons Hotel for lunch.

I'd been with Terrie for four and a half years by this point, and we'd seen some financial highs and lows, but we were really broke at this moment in time. I only had thirteen bucks and I needed breakfast in the morning, too, so I grabbed something cheap at McDonald's and then waited until it was time to head to the hotel. It must have been one of the hottest days of the year. I was sweating my dick off, and I could smell coke and booze oozing from my body. The hotel valet cost twenty bucks, so I had to park like eight blocks away and walk. By the time I got there, I had to sit in the lobby for ten minutes letting the sweat dry off before I could let them see my fat ass.

I finally got the nerve to walk in and saw Peter and Adam; it was terrifying. I could barely say a fucking word. I just sat there listening to them talk. I was stressed looking at the menu prices and finally landed on the steak medallions for thirty bucks. The entire time, all I could focus on was how I was going to pay my portion. On the chance they didn't pick up the check, I was fucked.

Luckily they paid, and luckily they liked me. I got the role. Terrie and I both cried—this was the answer to all of our problems. This movie was going to change *everything*.

They sent a limo for me for the table read and when I pulled up, I saw Adam standing there—among other huge stars—wearing a pair of flip flops and a fucking t-shirt. Right out of the gate, Adam showed what a down-to-earth guy he was. He even carried my luggage for Christ's sake. We ended up going immediately from the table read to a private plane and off to Santa Fe, New Mexico. We were set to film there for six weeks before heading back to Redondo Beach, California, for the second eleven-week part of the film's shoot.

The cast was insane; it was royalty. It was Burt Reynolds himself, a legend, Chris Rock, Steve Austin, Nick Turturro, Michael Irvin—all people over the years who I'd watched on TV and dreamed of working with, all there together in one room.

Plus, we were being treated like royalty, too. In Santa Fe, they brought us from the plane to a beautiful hotel. They'd rented out the entire thing for us. I got there with only thirty bucks and my driver's license, but at the hotel, they immediately gave me keys to my own Escalade to use while we were down there and they handed me eight hundred dollars as an initial payment for the week. I also got an immediate weed hookup, which was solid since I was trying to stay off coke while we were in Santa Fe. On set, they hired strippers to bring around smoothies and hold umbrellas for us in the sun.

Filming was hysterical. I got to work with Tracy Morgan, who was a specimen of comedy. He was such an inspiring guy: his style of comedy was funny off the cuff but crazy at the same time. The stuff that came out of his mouth made me look like a fucking child in the comedy game. Adam was great; that's the only way to describe him. He would rub my belly and tell me it reminded him of his father's belly. One day I had shorts on and my balls were hanging out—I didn't even realize—until he came over to me and said, "Hey, why don't you put that speed bag away?"

By the third week or so in Santa Fe, I'd gotten on the same wavelength as these guys. One day for a locker room scene, I felt comfortable enough to go up to Adam with a suggestion.

"Hey, Adam," I said walking up to him.

"What's up, Joey?"

"Listen, for this scene, I want to just wear a jockstrap . . . nothing else. I think it'll be funny, just like my big stomach hanging over the thing."

"I don't know, Adam," someone on set from Sony chimed in. "That doesn't sound like it's going to work."

"I think it could be funny," I continued. "Just my titties out and the whole thing."

After a few seconds, Adam shouted, "Get this man a jockstrap!"

It turned out to be one of the funniest scenes we shot down there. We were all just cracking each other up and having a fucking blast.

I got back on the coke when we got to Redondo Beach, but it wasn't fucking up my acting game, so I was fine with it. The way I saw it, nothing could bring me down from where I was at. In fact, things only went up. When the movie came out on Memorial Day weekend 2005, we had two big premieres: One in LA at the Chinese Theater and the other in New York City. The LA premiere was star-studded. People like Joe Montana, Cameron Crowe, Will Ferrell, and John C. Reilly were there, and then we all went to the after-party in Jimmy Kimmel's lot. They morphed the whole lot into a mini stadium with artificial turf, tables with footballs, and a goalpost. I'd never been to a premiere like that before, with a chocolate fountain and people walking around with any type of food you could imagine. When people talked about living the Hollywood life, this is what they meant. I couldn't have been happier.

Then, in New York City, I was able to bring seven of my childhood friends with me. I felt like this was my way of showing these guys that they hadn't made a bad choice by sticking by me all these years. All the bullshit they put up with was worth it. I was a big shot now, and they could come along for the ride.

I got *really* caught up in the moment. I thought I had arrived. See, the whole time we were filming, everyone was telling me that my phone would not stop ringing when this movie came out. On the flight home from the New York City premiere, I can't even describe the plans I had in my mind—these grandiose plans—that this was the end of my suffering and struggling. Now, I could pick and choose my roles. I knew my life would change from this movie. I was sure of it. I was going to be famous.

Hah!

The phone didn't ring. Nothing changed. The high of coming off a film like that to end up with no follow-up roles killed me. I felt like a failure again, like I'd felt for most of my life. I couldn't understand why this was happening—how I could go from such a high, then back to nothing. It consumed me whole.

In the two months after *The Longest Yard* came out, I only had one audition, and even that went terribly. The lady threw me out mid-audition because I was so out of it after a night of getting high. I guess I couldn't blame her.

On the comedy end, I was getting booked as a headliner now because people knew me from *The Longest Yard*—but just because I was booked as a headliner didn't mean I *was* a headliner. What I really was was a glorified feature act: a guy who should be opening for headliners. I didn't realize that until about three weeks in when I started noticing people were walking out of my shows. Literally getting up mid-set and walking the fuck out. They were coming to see the goofy guy from the movie, and when they got there, they saw a dirty comic who wasn't ready for prime time.

I'd get up onstage, and . . . *"So uhhh, yeah . . ."* I'd blank. Bottom line, I was never fully prepared. Not to mention, when I wasn't zoning out, my material was whack; it made no sense. I was taking my comedy for granted, and because of it, my shows were bad. As disappointment was really starting to set in, I set my sights on some new drugs to numb it.

I was doing a weekend of shows in Beaumont, Texas, and the guy who usually got me coke there had an offer I couldn't refuse.

"I can get you some Valium, too," he told me.

"Ehhh," I thought about it for a second. Even though I'd sold plenty of it in my day, I wasn't into that shit. But, what the fuck? I had friends in LA who'd buy it from me.

"How many you got?" I asked.

"Let's say, thirty."

I got so fucked up off Jägermeister shots and cocaine before my Friday night set that I completely blew it onstage. During the show, I was laying down on the stage, microphone on my chest, doing my jokes from there. At one point, I called out to my feature act for help.

"Josh, help me up on the stool."

I heard a yell from the back of the room. "No. Fuck you!"

Slowly over the weekend—in between a ton of coke—I started popping a Valium here and there. I'd have one, then two more a while later, then another. Then, I reached into the bag and there were none left. When I finally passed out—I was *out*.

I woke up to someone from the hotel pounding on my door telling me if I wanted to stay another day, it was forty bucks. I fell asleep again, and the next morning it was the same thing. I couldn't figure out how long I'd been cooped up in there. All I knew was my head was spinning. When I went into the bathroom, I noticed one entire side of my face was numb. I grabbed my phone and saw a ton of missed calls: Terrie, my friends, my agents, you name it.

It was Monday. I was supposed to be home by Sunday. I got ahold of Terrie and told her I was sick, leaving out what actually happened, and that I'd be home when I could. Then, I got ahold of a doctor in the area to look at my face. He said it would be fine, just needed a couple of days to come back to normal.

Those premieres for *The Longest Yard* were maybe the best I'd felt in my whole life. I'd been on top of the world, but even higher. Now, here I was, literally numbing myself, sliding back down, and even further down in certain ways than I'd ever been.

I was crushed.

22

How to Quit Cocaine

The first step to recovery for an addict is admitting you have a problem. I was no fucking fool—I knew I had a problem with cocaine. It was the other steps that tripped me up. Coke had become such a permanent fixture in my life—one I'd even been okay with keeping around to a certain extent—so quitting seemed impossible. By the time I was forty-three years old—not long after my downslide from *The Longest Yard*—and still a coke fiend, it started to become painful how badly I wanted to quit. But, I just couldn't.

I'd go three days with no coke. Then do it. Next time I'd make it four days. Then I'd slip up. I'd even make it five days in a row. But, then I was back at it. I watched as people I knew who were also addicts would go into rehab, get clean, and come out only to do *more* than ever before. I convinced myself I was different, but of course I wasn't. No matter how hard I tried, I couldn't shake it, and I was exhausted.

Still in my dark place after *The Longest Yard*, I found what felt like a ball on my neck, down near the clavicle. After a few weeks I noticed it was getting bigger and visible to the eye, too. My fear of what it could be started outweighing my fear of the doctor, so I went and had it checked out. Luckily, it wasn't cancerous, but the doctor said it still needed to come out.

"Listen, can I tell you something?" I asked the doctor, and he nodded. "I've got a bit of a drug problem. How's that going to affect the surgery?"

"Do me a favor," he said, "you can smoke weed, but don't do coke until after the surgery. Alright? It's going to have an impact, and we don't want a hard time with the anesthesia."

So you know what I did, right? Started partying even more. Now, I was regressing all the way back to my halfway house days. I did coke every night until the surgery, and tons of it. I couldn't stop.

I told my guy to have a bag of weed ready for me at lunchtime because my surgeon said I should be out of there by noon. I also called my coke dealer to get him ready, too. Then, I went to the bank and got four fifty-dollar bills. I folded the bills in squares and put them as far up my ass as I could. I didn't want any problems in the hospital, and I knew if you tipped the orderlies, they'd take care of you.

The surgery went fine, but when I woke up in recovery I was spooked. There were tons of people I didn't know around me, and I kept mentally flashing back to a time I'd watched *Apocalypse Now* on acid. I started freaking out, ripping my wires off.

"I need to get the fuck out of here!" I screamed. "I need air, I can't breathe in here!"

The doctor came in quickly.

"Hey, Joey, calm down, alright," he said. "Just calm down. The surgery went well. You're okay."

Once I chilled out a little, he continued. "The mass was bigger than we expected, so we had to break your collarbone to get it out. But you're fine. Do you want to see it?"

When he walked back in with a ball of pus the size of a softball, I lost it again. To me, it represented a mass of everything bad I'd done to my body over the years—the drugs, the booze. I jumped up and ran down the hall. The nurses were chasing me, Terrie was chasing me, and I just kept moving with the IV stand still attached. I noticed an orderly standing there with a wheelchair, and I pulled a fifty out of my ass crack and asked him for a lift.

He got me in the wheelchair, and we were off to my car. I handed him more cash outside and gave him a hug as I saw Terrie running up, white as a ghost.

"Terrie, I'm sorry," I said. "I just need to leave this fucking place."

Despite how embarrassed she was, she agreed to make the couple of stops for me—thinking both were weed pick-ups—and I was set for a few days. Every time I'd sneak to our garage to do a line (I thought it was bad luck to do coke *in* the apartment), I'd snort, a stitch would pop, and blood would come out of the wound. When I got a call to read for *Hannah Montana* a few days later, the casting director was horrified.

"Is that blood on your neck?" He stopped me mid-line, blood dripping down my chest.

I didn't get that part.

I'd gotten a Vicodin prescription after the surgery, and they were going down like candy. When the first bottle was gone, the doctor prescribed more, and then the damage was done. This shit took me to a weird place. I kept withdrawing. I knew the end was near for me, and I mean that. I was overweight, smoking cigarettes, my diet was bad, and my attitude was bad. I'd really given up on myself.

One day I got a call from a buddy back in Jersey. His brother, a guy we called Bonehead—a tall, dark and handsome dude who was just a sweetheart of a guy—was now on heroin. He was what we'd call a productive addict. He had a successful plumbing business but still managed to squeeze in time for his habit. I loved the guy and his family, though, and when he told me the price of heroin had plummeted there since 9/11, he asked if I'd be interested.

"It's real cheap, like three dollars a bag, if you want some," he told me one afternoon.

I'd tried heroin maybe twice in my life. I saw the life of a junkie, and I didn't want that. Years back when I'd briefly lived with my buddy in New Jersey, he'd developed a heroin addiction. His grandma lived with us, too, and her favorite saying was, "What the fuck is going on?" She was always screaming it. She loved her cats—had about four of them—and at night he would wait until she got in bed (always with the cats) before he'd shoot up in the bathroom. A few minutes after he'd be in there, I'd make the loudest sound I could to wake up Grandma. She'd come running out of her room, screaming, "What the fuck is going on?" as my friend hid in the bathroom, cursing me off.

It was funny as fuck but also sad looking back. If I thought I had to be sneaky with coke, my friend's entire life was sneaking around with heroin like that. It seemed stressful, not to mention he was always just *out of it* when he was on the shit. I knew plenty of other people who did heroin, too, and there was something about that drug and what it did to people that just bothered me.

But, on the phone with Bonehead that day, I just didn't fucking care anymore.

"Fuck it," I said. "Send me a couple of bags."

I heard a rumor if you do heroin two or three days in a row, you get addicted, so I decided to only snort it on Mondays. I'd get high and sleep for a day and a half, puke, the whole thing. I kept it up for a few weeks and then realized I'd stopped doing coke, without really meaning to. I didn't do coke for that whole summer. In my addict mind, I thought I found the cure for cocaine addiction: heroin. I even wrote a letter to the producers of *60 Minutes* telling them I'd found the cure to the cocaine epidemic: just do a line of heroin and your urge for coke will start to fade.

My new hobby aside, that summer Terrie and I somehow ended up with an entire colony of stray cats in our backyard. We had like fifteen kittens back there at a time. Two of the siblings we called Superbad and DJ. DJ was a beautiful Siamese cat with blue eyes. Superbad, on the other hand, was a daredevil and always getting DJ into trouble. Superbad and I didn't get along at all.

By the fall, I somehow managed to switch from heroin back to coke, and I was going wild. Then, something fucking tragic happened. Marilyn Martinez got sick. She'd become one of my closest friends by then. She was diagnosed with stage four cancer, and they gave her a couple of months to live, maybe a year. I was devastated.

She was in the hospital for a while, but when they sent her home, I went over to talk to her one day.

"How are you feeling?" I asked at her bedside.

"Better, I think," she said. "If I beat this cancer, I'm never going to be a dirty comic again. I don't want to have to answer for it when I see God."

I started laughing.

"Hey," she looked me straight in the eye. "God wants you to stop doing coke."

Her words hit me like a kick to the balls. We'd never had a conversation like this before.

"Okay," I finally responded. "I'm hearing you."

I had a comedy show coming up in Jersey, and I wanted to listen to her words, to give it a trial run. I got to Jersey on a Thursday, didn't do any coke, then Friday night didn't do it either. When I got back to my room Friday night, I got a call: Marilyn had died.

Why did God always need to take the people I cared most about?

I was heartbroken, and I had to honor Marilyn's wishes; I knew that. I stayed clean the whole weekend and when I got back to LA, I had a meeting for a movie I'd previously done a table read for.

"The role is yours if you want it," the casting director said to me almost immediately. "We actually brought you here to talk about something else."

"Okay . . ."

"This movie is going to shoot twenty-one days straight, no breaks."

"Okay," I repeated.

"We know you like to party, Joey," he said. "This shoot isn't going to allow for that. If you don't show up on time or fuck up, you'll screw over everyone on this production. Are you understanding?"

"I'm hearing you."

"Go home and think about it . . . really think about it, and then let us know if you can do it."

I walked out of that meeting fucking hot. I was mad at them for calling me out on my problem, but I was madder at myself. This whole time, I thought I was shucking and jiving and nobody knew about my problem. It turns out, the whole industry knew.

I ended up agreeing to the movie. All I needed to do was focus on my commitment to Marilyn.

Later that week we had Marilyn's memorial at The Store. I don't know if it was the coke withdrawals or just the fact that I hate fucking funerals, but I was on edge. When they told me I was first to get up and speak, I couldn't wait to get it over with.

When I took the mic and looked out into the crowd, I froze for a second. Standing in the back with a smug look and a mouth full of free food was a booker who had made it a game to torture Marilyn. He'd offer her spots on a popular comedy festival only to call her back and say that it was a no-go because her act was too dirty. And then he'd add a dirty show to the festival and not invite her to perform. He played with her like this for years.

How dare he show his face at her memorial? Needless to say, I went off, and by the time I was done, he was long gone. I walked offstage in a daze, and it hit me: I stood up for a friend, the same way Zoraida did for my mom. Except without the blow.

Don't get me wrong, I had some. On me. I'd bought a gram on the way and promised myself it would be my last ever. But I ended up giving it to a friend later that night instead of doing it. I still wanted my last hoorah, so a few nights later I did the same thing: bought some coke and told myself the last I'd ever do would be after my set that night at The Store. But when I got offstage, I got a call from Terrie.

"Joey, the kittens are sick." She was crying. "Superbad and DJ, they're going to die."

The cats had anemia. By the time I rushed home, they weren't in good shape at all. They were both in the bathroom, and throughout the night, every time I'd go in there I'd pet DJ but wouldn't touch Superbad. I did some of the coke in there, too—the first time I'd ever, *ever* done it in the apartment.

At around 7 AM, Terrie woke me up.

"DJ died," she told me, crying.

All I could think was that it was my fault. I'd brought the coke inside, and now my favorite cat was dead. I knew better than to bring the fucking coke inside! I thought about Superbad. He was a prick, but I really didn't want him to die. Terrie made some oatmeal cookies, and

I got on my hands and knees and started feeding him little pieces of the cookies—bit by bit—in the bathroom. I looked up and I said, "God, as much as I hate this cat, if you save him, I will never do cocaine again."

That fucking cat—he survived. Keeping my word to Marilyn and God, I never did cocaine again. Ever. I mean it.

Once I was able to quit cocaine for good, I started to change other parts of my life for the better, too. I got into the gym, started Weight Watchers, and over time dropped nearly a hundred and fifty pounds. I also managed to reconnect with my Uncle Lazaro. I was out in Malibu on an audition and stopped to eat a sandwich on the rocks looking out at the ocean when it hit me: I'd been to the exact spot with Uncle Lazaro when I was a kid. I decided to call him.

It had been twenty-five years since we'd spoken—twenty-five years since we'd pulled guns on each other—but once we talked, all was forgiven.

"I was in bad shape back then," I told him. "I didn't realize I was still grieving my mother, but I was hurting bad. I was on a lot of drugs, and I don't expect you to accept my apology, but I'm very sorry for what I did and how I acted."

"I'm sorry, too, Joey," he said. "I was in a bad place, too. I had a mistress and was cheating on her with her cousin, and things got very complicated. I didn't know how to deal with it except act like an asshole."

We ended up getting together at his bar, the very same one he'd owned back then, and caught up. From then on, we got together for weekly lunches and the occasional Dodgers game. It was amazing to have family back in my life.

Clean of the cocaine and on the right track, I solidified Terrie as family, too. What I had with Terrie was realer than anything I'd ever experienced with any other woman. It was love like I'd never known before. So when she visited her family one weekend out in Tennessee to meet her new nephew and came back a little bummed, I knew she was feeling some kind of way. She deserved happiness, and I wanted to give it to her.

"Will you marry me, Terrie?" I asked her over the phone while she was at work.

"What?" She was as surprised as I was. "What made you change your mind?"

"I just want to marry you," I said. "And, I already called your dad and asked for your hand in marriage."

"You did?" Her tone was more upbeat now than I'd heard it in days.

"Yes . . . so what do you think?"

"Okay, Joey, I'll marry you."

Our wedding was simple, just the way we wanted it. We planned the ceremony at a local chapel on the Wednesday before Thanksgiving in 2009. By then, Terrie had moved to an accounting job at The Hollywood Bowl—wanting a change from waitressing and having grown tired of the acting scene in LA—and they gifted us a reception. There was no dress code, no gifts required, we just wanted our people there to celebrate and have fun.

Everything I felt on my wedding day, and every day since, felt like the best decision I ever made. Thank God for that.

And thank fucking God to be free of cocaine. My life was truly turned around.

23

The Church of What's Happening Now

T hat's the most disturbing thing I've ever heard," Felicia Michaels, a fellow comic, said to me, tears welled up in her eyes. She was sitting across from me at her microphone while we recorded an episode of our podcast, *Beauty and Da Beast*. Her jaw dropped in horror as I told what was, truly, very disturbing.

The story went like this: Back in the '80s, my friends and I were out in New York City one night, and my buddy Roger wanted a blow job before we called the night quits. In the early '80s, there had to be two hundred hookers outside of the Lincoln Tunnel every night. The Lower West Side was a hooker haven. The streets would be lined with cars and hookers, all guarded by a homeless guy in a wheelchair who carried a machine gun in case there was trouble.

We got Roger set up, and our friend Alfie volunteered to be on look-out near the car while Stinky and I walked down the street to grab a couple of what we called "cancer pretzels" (the pretzels they sold by the tunnel were filled with carbon monoxide; you could get dizzy just eating them). When we got back to the car twenty minutes later, Roger and the hooker were still in there, car bouncing.

"What the fuck is taking so long?" Stinky asked.

We stood there listening and heard Roger in the car saying, "You're not sucking it right . . ."

"I think she wants to come back to Jersey with us," Alfie said. "Let's just get in."

We hopped in the car, and she kept doing her thing. Then, we started driving. It was a couple of blocks before this lady popped her head up.

"Where the fuck are we going?" she screamed.

"Back to Jersey," Alfie said.

"I don't want to go to Jersey," the hooker said.

We argued back and forth going through the tunnel before she whipped out a straight razor. We grabbed her arm so she wouldn't cut us, and as we were doing that, her wig came off. We got to the Jersey side, razor in her hand and wig in mine, everyone yelling. We pulled over at a cemetery and told her to get out of the car and give us her money. She spread her legs and pulled out sixty bucks in crumpled up cash. She kept cursing while she threw the money at us. Her purse had fallen out all over the car and condoms, perfume, and a ton of other shit dumped out. I cleaned it up to give back to her, then held up her wig, lit it on fire, and tossed it to her. She stamped out the fire and put the wig right back on her head like no big fucking deal.

Telling this story publicly was a huge risk, I knew that. This was my ugly past, and I was living my life very differently now. But I went for it—dick on the table—and didn't sugarcoat anything. I had no clue how the listeners would react.

Our podcast came to be in 2010 after I'd done some soul-searching on what was next for me. I wanted something outside of the box. Felicia and I had been friends a while, and when we kept running into each other at a local coffee shop, we got to talking. While we were both in the process of brainstorming our next steps for comedy, we thought, why not combine forces?

"Have you ever thought about doing a podcast?" she asked me one day. "With the kind of traction some of these comedians are getting with theirs, it seems like something that could really work."

I knew exactly what she meant, too. Every time I went on Joe Rogan's podcast as a guest, I'd see my Twitter following jump up a couple of thousand followers. Adam Carolla and Marc Maron had really popular podcasts then, too, so it seemed like something worth exploring.

"What if we did it together?" I asked her, and she immediately agreed.

We both chipped in like a hundred forty bucks for equipment, and we were off. The podcasting world was fairly new, but with her being an experienced comedian and an absolute sweetheart, and me being a savage, we thought our dynamic could really stir things up. We met every Tuesday, talked for a half hour or so, then started recording. Then, we'd put it up on Thursdays. We avoided current events—we wanted people to be able to listen to this thing thirty years in the future and still find it relevant—but otherwise we would just shoot the shit.

Incorporating my life stories into my comedy—in the podcast and onstage—was without a doubt getting me the best comedy results of my life. It was becoming my thing. For inspiration with it, I started watching old Howard Stern interviews with Artie Lange. I noticed that Artie had this style of telling stories that was fucking captivating. The best part was, no matter how ridiculous and fucked-up the stories were,

Artie just sat there telling his bitter truth. It's what gave me the nerve to tell that hooker story. I knew it could end my career, but I needed to put it out there.

When that story went live, my Twitter blew up—followers were coming out of the woodwork saying how funny they thought it was. I couldn't believe it. A couple of weeks after telling it, I had a stand-up gig and I was running late. The club owner called me on my way there.

"Joey, you gotta get down here right away," he said.

"I'm coming. What's up?"

"We have a hundred and fifty people here waiting for you."

Even after my spike from *The Longest Yard* as the "headliner," I never had a hundred and fifty people come out to a club for me. When I got there, the crowd was begging for the hooker story. They ate it up. These people were interested in hearing my kind of comedy—dirty and off-color. From one stupid fucking story, our podcast started growing and I gained a real fan base, or as I like to call them, *family*.

I'd been adding storytelling into my stand-up for a while, but now I started to monopolize on the fact that these people loved hearing the crazy shit I'd done in my life. I started keeping notes on the funny stuff from my past and figuring out the craziest ways to tell them onstage and beyond.

One day I got an email from a recent college graduate named Lee Syatt who liked what I was doing with *Beauty and Da Beast* and had some ideas for me. Lee was a little, round Jewish kid who was very funny and very smart, and when he got worked up, a neurotic, stuttering mess. He started working with me a little, taking videos from the road and editing them for YouTube. I liked Lee a lot because he wasn't like any of the other pricks in LA: this guy wasn't looking to be a star or any of that shit, all he wanted was a job. We had a thirty-year age gap, but we became quick friends.

"I think the world is ready for you on your own now," Lee said to me candidly after a few months of working together.

"You think so?" I wasn't sure, but at the same time, Felicia and I had been in a weird spot, growing apart a little. I loved her to death, but I also knew the stories I started telling were becoming a little *too much* for her. I knew it, and she knew it. After 113 episodes of *Beauty and Da Beast*, we decided to end it in November 2012. Despite our creative differences, we remain friends to this day.

That same year, Lee and I started a podcast in the spare bedroom at a new place Terrie and I had moved into. We called our podcast *The Church of What's Happening Now*. Lee was only interested in producing it; he didn't want to be on air at all, but eventually that changed. One morning I had him smoke weed out of a pipe I'd made from a Coke can, and the kid almost had a heart attack. He didn't really smoke back then, let alone at six in the morning when we got together for the production. His face got all red, and he had to sit down while I gave him water to chill him out. When we talked about it on air, the reaction we got was tremendous. That was when the character Lee was born.

Meanwhile, my buddy Ari Shaffir had something cooking that was right up that alley. He was starting a storytelling show called *Psychedelia*—which later became *This Is Not Happening*—and wanted me to perform in it.

On the night of the recording, I told a story off the cuff about when I was sixteen years old at a Pink Floyd concert with my friends. We were all too young to drive, but we got connected with this dude called Satan—not to be confused with The Devil—who could help us get up to Nassau Coliseum.

Satan was just like you'd expect him to be—he had that fucking *look* in his eyes. I didn't know much about him except that he'd gotten thrown out of the marines . . . this guy was hardcore. The whole ride up to the show he was telling us how he wanted to kill people, his mother included since she'd taken his weed from him. Satan was weaving through traffic at ninety miles per hour, smoking a joint and drinking a beer.

We all did a ton of acid that night so we were tripping fucking hard, and if Satan's eyes weren't bad enough to begin with, those eyeballs would burn a hole through you now. We had these cute, innocent chicks sitting by us at the concert, and I could tell Satan was just watching them, scaring the fuck out of them with that look. Then, during one of Pink Floyd's intermissions, balloons were getting shot out everywhere, and Satan took out his lighter and was popping them screaming "POP!" every time.

When one of the girls asked him what he was doing, he looked into her soul and said, "Satan does not like balloons." I've never seen people evacuate from their seats quicker than they did.

The audience at Ari's show went nuts for the story, and when the video somehow made it to YouTube, my Twitter blew up even more. Again, people wanted more.

On *The Church*, Lee and I just kept being ourselves. We'd both get high, and I'd hope Lee would say something weird, and I would torture him a little. It became our routine. We were wrecked doing these podcasts, totally blasted on weed or some sort of psychedelic. And we had no clue what we were creating here—a devoted audience of followers—we were just a couple of dudes having a fucking blast. Over time, we went from a few thousand downloads to up to 500,000 downloads per episode.

One night, I got a call from the manager at an improv in Irvine saying the scheduled comic for the night cancelled, and he wanted to see if I could fill in. I said yes, and Lee came with me.

"You want me to tape your set tonight?" he asked on our drive over.

"Actually, good thinking," I told him. "Definitely."

I was super relaxed onstage that night—I did a bunch of new material and improvised a lot—and it turned out to be a perfect set, which rarely happened. It came out perfect on tape, too. Lee and I both looked at each other with the same thought: this is a fucking album.

A connection at Apple helped us put it together. We titled it *It's Either You or The Priest*, and within hours of going up, it became No. 1 on the iTunes comedy charts.

I'd been doing comedy for nineteen years by then, and at last, I finally started to feel like I'd made a real name for myself. I mostly thank *The Church*.

24

Second Chances

I experienced a lot of letdowns in my life, particularly my mother's death. Finding her body—losing a parent in that way—haunted me for years, crept up on me in the moments I'd least expect it way down the road. The loss helped define me as a thief and an addict throughout my life, even though I denied that it did. My mother told me to be a man, and when opportunities had come to do it, I'd failed—sometimes despite my best efforts.

Losing a daughter crept up on me in a similar way. The circumstances may have been different, but the loss hurt all the same. For a while after I left Colorado, I'd write letters to Jackie or send pictures, and Kathy would swear up and down they didn't get them. Jackie never seemed to get my gifts, either. My voicemails were never returned. Eventually I found out they'd up and moved to England. I knew in that moment that she was officially gone—no longer a part of me at all. I'll never forget when I found out they'd moved overseas. I got on my hands and knees and prayed to God to help me get past this situation. I knew I was not a father anymore, and all I wanted was for Jackie to grow up in peace. I had been the only person trying to keep my relationship with her alive—no fault of hers, she was just a kid—but I couldn't do it anymore. I would love my daughter forever, and keep my heart open, but I needed to try to move forward, given the circumstances. I had to put it to bed, for everyone's sake.

But the pain of losing her still wouldn't subside, and it never really did.

Then, by a fucking miracle, I got a second chance at fatherhood.

"I have to tell you something, Joey," Terrie said to me when she got home from church on Mother's Day in 2012. I could tell whatever she was about to say was big, and I was right.

"I'm pregnant."

"Are you fucking serious?" I said, practically jumping up. I was thrilled.

"I'm serious," she said, smiling from ear to ear. I'd never seen her look so happy.

We'd been together for twelve years and never even had a close call, and now out of nowhere, we were having a baby. It wasn't until we got home from a barbecue later that night that it hit me like a ton of bricks. I was forty-nine years old. Terrie was in her forties, too. And we were having a kid?

I was down for a couple of days. I had this weird feeling that I hadn't felt in a while. It was a huge deal to become a father again, and considering I'd failed so badly at it the first time, what were my chances of succeeding at it now? But, the reality was this: I was more mature and healthier, and I had my shit together, a steady income, a job I was fucking good at and loved. My first marriage had tanked, but what I had with Terrie was fucking tremendous, proof that history didn't always repeat itself. I was determined to do this father thing right. Terrie and I were going to bring that kid into the world, and it would be the best thing to ever happen in my life.

I was right.

On January 8, 2013, Terrie gave birth to our beautiful baby girl at the Kaiser hospital in Hollywood. We named her Mercy. Our own little LA Woman. I can't tell you the amount of happiness and peace this kid brought into my life. As a dad now—free of a cocaine habit and without the urge to rob and rip off everyone I encountered—I could do it right. I'd live my life *for* this little girl.

"I promise to give you the best life possible," I whispered, holding her for the first time. And I meant it.

With Mercy in my life, I had an overwhelming sense that I needed to try to speak to Jackie again. I wanted to hear her voice, find out how she was, learn about her life. I wanted to tell her and her mother that I'd finally cleaned up my act—this time for real—and I'd become someone Jackie would *want* in her life. I found a number for them, called, and left a message. A few days later the phone rang, and it was Kathy.

"How have you been, Joey?" she asked, kindly. I was pleasantly surprised at her tone.

"I've been really good, yeah, actually *really* good."

I told her everything, including that I had another daughter now, too, and how I'd been happily married for a few years. She said she'd seen the success I was having in my career and congratulated me. She even said she was *happy* for me. I was shocked. Then she asked point blank: "Does your wife know you're a junkie?"

"Listen, Kathy, that's all in the past," I told her. "I don't mess with any of that stuff anymore. I just smoke pot now, that's it."

"You could never get off that shit," she said, not buying it. "No way. That's what you'd always say, and then you'd be right back on it."

For all the good things she led with in our conversation, there were plenty of bad things to match them by the end.

"I understand how you feel and I'm sorry for what happened in the past," I apologized. "But, truthfully, I'm a different man now."

I don't fault Kathy at all for acting like she did—I wouldn't let Mercy be with the man I was in my twenties. By the end of the call, Kathy let me know Jackie was going through a tough time—her grandfather had just died and she was going through a breakup—but Kathy thought it would be nice for her and me to catch up.

"Let me relay the message to her, and I'm sure she'll give you a call in the next couple of days," Kathy said.

I never heard from them again. Weirdly enough, that was really okay with me this time . . . *finally*. After all the years of anguish over it, I was finally able to accept the situation for what it was. I'd messed up my chance to be Jackie's dad all of those years ago, and they didn't believe I deserved a second chance. But, the truth was, I had one with Mercy—and it was about as great as could be.

Other aspects of my life were coming full circle, too. For a few years, every time I'd do a show in Arizona, I'd try to get Rome Madden to show up because he lived around there. I fucking kidnapped the dude, so I knew it was a long shot, but I wanted to make formal, in-person amends. I'd done a public apology on *The Church of What's Happening Now*, but I figured if I could see the guy, give him a hug, and tell him how sorry I really was, I could finally put it all behind me. After seven years of asking, he finally came to a Tucson show. We talked, we hugged, we cried—and I apologized from the bottom of my heart. It was great to see him, and a fucking weight lifted off my shoulders.

On the acting side, when I'd gotten to work with Robert De Niro on *Analyze That*, it was 2002, and fuck was I in a different place then.

So when I got offered a second opportunity to work with him—and Sylvester fucking Stallone—in *Grudge Match*, I was excited to do it as the clean version of myself. This time around, I even got to work one-on-one with De Niro; he was as nice and fucking cool as everyone says he is. He even took tips from me on how to make some of his lines funnier.

When *Grudge Match* came out on Christmas Day 2013, I was hit with a whole new part of the experience. I was so fired up about the movie coming out. I told my podcast listeners to show up to the North Hollywood theater I was going to be at for the 8 PM screening, and to get there early so I could smoke pot with them outside. I expected maybe ten or fifteen people to show up. When I got there, there were over a hundred people waiting. They all started clapping, and we all hung out in a giant cloud of smoke. It was like an impromptu premiere. I get fucking chills sometimes even thinking about it.

On the comedy side, for a few years leading up to 2014, I'd stopped performing at The Comedy Store. The place had turned dark. If you were a comic in LA during that time, you know what I mean. Then in 2014, a guy named Adam Eget came on as the new talent coordinator, and he called me to say they wanted me back. I wasn't sure what to say initially; I told him I needed some time to think.

I was about to get a colonoscopy, and if you've ever gotten one, you know the shit that pours out of your ass the night before from those laxatives is fucking brutal. You're basically glued to the can. You can't sleep at all. In the middle of that sleepless night, a movie came on with Peter Sellers. It had been one of Marilyn Martinez's favorites. By the end, I was crying. This was definitely a sign from Marilyn that I needed to go back to The Store, and I trusted anything Marilyn would direct me to do. So I told Adam yes.

I got up onstage, and . . . *"It's great to be back at the world-famous fucking Comedy Store!"*

That first night, I could tell it was the old Store again. The building was alive—you felt the energy as soon as you walked in the door. It was a *holy fuck* feeling because as much as things were the same, they were also different. I was a seasoned professional now. People were coming to *me* for advice on their stand-up. The comics knew and respected me, and my fans were selling out rooms because they wanted to hear my material. Now I was the elder in the game, and I started to talk to the younger comics like a mentor. I'd really become Uncle Joey.

In the years after that, I'd go on to amp up my comedy game even more. I got to do comedy specials, like a back-to-back special with Doug Stanhope for an NBC channel and a thirty-minute special for Netflix's *The Degenerates.* I started selling out fifteen-hundred-seat theaters, something I never even dreamed of. I got spots on Funny or Die's Odd-ball Comedy & Curiosity Festival Tour with Dane Cook and Sebastian Maniscalco. And, *The Church* was thriving. My social media following continued to blow up. I was getting on stages, writing, evolving, smoking ninety-two pounds of weed a week, eating I don't even know how many edibles, and working like a fucking savage.

I'd built myself a comedy career out of nothing, had dozens of acting gigs under my belt—working with some of the top names in the industry—and built a family of loyal fans. People were recognizing me on the street, asking for my autograph, and wanting to take pictures with me. I'd made it, and on my own terms. Best of all, I'd married the love of my life, brought an amazing kid into the world, and started a real home.

Truth be told, I was proud of myself. And I knew I'd become a version of myself that my mother could be proud of, too. That felt fucking tremendous.

And that, my friends, is the story of your Uncle Joey.

AFTERWORD

I n the summer of 2020, I sat on the steps of The Comedy Store with Terrie and Mercy, reflecting. The doors were locked—everything closed up because of Covid-19—so we couldn't go in, but we didn't need to. We just needed to sit quietly for a few minutes, soaking it all in before we left town. We explained to Mercy how important that place was for us: how her mom and I would have never met if it wasn't for that place, and how she would have never existed. I told her how my entire career—and life as a whole—changed for the better because of The Comedy Store.

Mitzi Shore had died a few years earlier, so it was easier to say goodbye than it would have been otherwise. I made sure to silently thank her and The Store for treating me as well as they did. Because it really was goodbye now. We were set to head off to New Jersey, back to my roots, to raise our daughter there.

We first talked about moving East during a Christmastime trip the three of us took in 2017. Terrie and I wanted to show Mercy what New York City was like around the holidays, and we saw it all: the Rockettes at Radio City Music Hall, the tree, Bryant Park to see the ice skaters, and St. Patrick's Cathedral, and ate at some great Chinese and Italian restaurants. I could tell my wife was a different person when we were there. Her eyes were extra shiny. She loved everything about New York City.

On the way home, as we were about to board our plane, Terrie held me back for a second.

"Give me a good reason why we should get on that plane," she said to me.

"What?" I asked, shocked.

"I just wish we lived here," she continued. She had tears in her eyes, so I knew she was serious. She didn't want to leave. "Aren't you ready to come back?" she asked me.

"You know what, I think I am," I said, and I meant it.

Then a couple of years later in 2019, I landed a role in *The Many Saints of Newark*, the prequel to *The Sopranos*. After many years of trying to get a role on *The Sopranos*, I was fucking pumped, especially to work with David Chase. The film shot in New York City for three weeks, then I had ten days off, and then I was back to New York City for another two weeks. It gave me time to reacquaint myself with my home turf, with my childhood. I couldn't get enough.

When I got back to Los Angeles, I told Terrie, "Okay, let's do it. Let's get out of LA."

Don't get me wrong, LA had been tremendous to me. But, over time I was getting burned out and losing steam. I made a promise when Mercy was born to be the best father I could be for her, and it was becoming harder and harder to do as an LA comic. I dreamed of a life for us that was traditional beyond LA standards, in a little community, where Mercy had her group of friends and played sports, and life felt *normal*.

Being on the road so much took that time away from us. The travel that comes with comedy is a big-time mental game, and it takes a toll. By the holidays in 2019, I tried explaining to my manager how wiped I was. I told him how I wanted to take a break from the road, but it seemed to be going in one ear and out the other. All I wanted was a breather and to be able to spend more time with my family.

Then, that New Year's, my insides fell apart when Mercy said to me straight up, "You have to start being home more, Dad."

I felt that through my fucking soul. I promised her things would change, and I wasn't kidding. I'd already lost my family in the past. I couldn't lose another family now. From then on, getting off the road, out of LA, and back to the East Coast was my goal.

I got to thinking a lot about my buddy Ralphie May, who'd passed away at only forty-five years old. He died of cardiac arrest, and I thought of it as a broken heart. I saw how the last years were so grueling for him; how much sadness he started to have with how his life was going, and how work—the travel, the hours—was eating him alive. It reminded me of my mom and the end of her life; she was also taken way too soon. I didn't want that to ever happen to me. I wanted to live the happiest life I could, and like Tony Bennett said, I wanted to be around.

The day Kobe Bryant died in January 2020, I was coming back from a couple of shows out in Atlanta, and when I landed at LAX, I had this creepy, eerie feeling. I'd heard about something happening in China but didn't understand the severity of it yet, but I noticed some people in the airports wearing masks. I swear that day in LA was cloudy and gray, not California gray, but East Coast gray. The wind was even weird. It felt like Halloween day in Jersey. You could tell something was off, and when we found out about Kobe, I assumed that was it.

But that creepy feeling kept following me.

In early March 2020, I was doing The Store, and when I got there, people were talking about this idea of "social distancing." By this point, Covid talk was everywhere, and I was fucking freaked out. I stood in the corner waiting to go onstage, did my twenty minutes, and felt that creepy feeling lingering there with me the whole time. I told them I wasn't feeling good, cancelled my second set, and went home. Little did I know that would be the last time I set foot inside The Comedy Store.

It was a confusing and scary time. The only thing I could do to try to keep some semblance of normalcy was record our podcast like usual, now in a proper studio across from a funeral home. Other than that, I was just focused on staying alive. I'd had bouts of terrible anxiety for years, but now I was having little panic attacks a few times a day. Everything about the pandemic was attacking my psyche.

Then, I started seeing things around town that I hadn't seen in thirty years. The shit was right out of a fucking movie: a dude fist fighting a hooker outside of my CVS, a dude on Main Street and Lankershim Boulevard in the middle of the road hitting people with a two-by-four at 2:30 in the afternoon, the homeless population doubling, gangs tagging our park and Mercy's school. I started carrying a gun on me at all times because I didn't know what was going to happen.

If I wasn't sure when I'd been filming *The Many Saints of Newark*, I was sure as fuck now—we needed to leave. I made a call to a comic friend of mine, Jim Florentine, who lived in New Jersey and asked if he knew of a good realtor to find us something in his area, and quick. He hooked us up with his sister-in-law, and sooner than we knew it, she found us the perfect house there. We were all set.

Leaving LA, I also made the difficult decision to end *The Church of What's Happening Now*. Lee and I had built something fucking beautiful together. We had a reach that neither of us even knew would be possible, but together we did it. I'm forever grateful to Lee for our eight years together on *The Church*. Those were some of the best times of my life.

On the steps of The Comedy Store on one of our last days in LA, we knew we'd made the right decision. I'm sure I'll be back there one day—I can never seem to get away from that place—but for now, we were off.

On that plane ride to New Jersey, all I could think of was my mom's words to me: *"Be a man."* When I left New Jersey in 1985, I had no intention of ever moving back. I'd left there a bum, a loser. I had nothing good in my life. I'd burned every bridge possible. But now I'd earned my place there. I was coming back to my roots a completely different person—my family along with me—and with my dignity.

I came back to New Jersey a man.

—Joey "Coco" Diaz

ACKNOWLEDGMENTS

To anyone who reads this book, yes, I've had a crazy life. I never thought I'd make it past the age of 37, and I never thought I'd amount to anything. I always thought that I would die in a jail cell or on a street because that was what my life meant to me.

That all changed in the summer of 2000 when I met a young, sweet girl named Terrie Clark. She was from Tennessee and we basically had nothing in common. She was a waitress at The World-Famous Comedy Store and I was a flunky comic. When we locked eyes . . . it was magic! Although there was a problem—I was a junkie ex-felon who had no future—she didn't see it that way. She took me in as the stray dog that I was. We dated for a few months, then I moved in—I was wild and crazy at the time, but little by little, her love crept in. It took me a while but then I realized the woman that I had, and I took control of my life. I was sick of letting people down and I made a decision never to let her down . . . and here we are.

I want to thank my wife for giving me the strength to reach my goals and to write this book. Thank you for the life you've provided for me and our beautiful daughter . . . Till the wheels fall off.

As far as my comedy career, I'd like to give special thanks to Richard Pryor for opening up my mind and for letting me know that it's alright to be yourself. Andrew "Dice" Clay for getting me off my ass and making me realize the dream was real. Jimmy Abeyta, Todd Jordan, and The Comedy Works in Denver for giving me the opportunity. Josh Wolf, Carl Warmenhoven, Ron Reid, Rod Long, Rick Ducommun, and The Comedy Underground in Seattle for letting me develop. And without Mitzi Shore and Paul Mooney, where would I be? They guided me in different ways, and I'll always be in their debt. The lessons they taught me were invaluable, and I hope to pass them on to keep their memory alive. Joe Rogan, you fucking animal . . . thank you for the brotherly love and for letting me know that I was a Savage! Ari Shaffir and Duncan Trussell for being my Comedy Store brothers and to my podcast mentor, Brian Redban, for letting me spread my stories to the world.

I'd love to thank Union City, New Jersey, for introducing me to my culture and for the education that I learned at my mother's bar. It was the foundation of my comedy if you really think about it. I'd also like to thank North Bergen, New Jersey, for the education and love that I gathered there. Without those families, I wouldn't be here today: the Benders, the Runnes, the Balzanos, the Ascoleses, Mr. Barone for being my friend when I needed one, and Mr. Terranova for saving my life. Thank you to the Vilanos, the Contys, the Tabascos, the Lubranos, the Quinteros, the Avillos, and the Holloways. Jimmy Burkle, thank you for showing me a different way. I miss you dearly. Mike Duffy, you fucking nut! And a special thank you to my brother George K, you and your family were the bomb!

Anthony Balzano and Dominick Speciale . . . there's not a day that goes by that I don't think of you. I'll always keep your memory alive.

If I missed anyone, I'm sorry . . . You know I love you dearly!

ABOUT THE AUTHOR

Joey "Coco" Diaz is a Cuban-American actor, comedian, podcast host, husband, and father. Diaz was born in Cuba and immigrated to the United States at age three. Orphaned in his teenage years, Diaz ventured into the world of crime and landed himself in jail for kidnapping, before changing his life around and finding his true calling with comedy. Diaz's comedy career later moved him to Los Angeles, where he snagged his first role on the big screen in the sports comedy film *BASEketball*. He continued acting with roles in TV series including *NYPD Blue* and *My Name is Earl* and went on to appear in films such as *Analyze That*, *Spider-Man 2*, *The Longest Yard*, and most recently, *The Many Saints of Newark*. Diaz's comedy career gained major traction with his popular podcast *The Church of What's Happening Now* and his regular appearances on *The Joe Rogan Experience*. Diaz now hosts the twice-weekly podcast *Uncle Joey's Joint*.